T

ORIGINS, PHILOSOPHY, PRACTICE

The Martial Arts

ORIGINS, PHILOSOPHY, PRACTICE

PETER LEWIS

PRION

Revised edition first published
in Great Britain 1996 by Prion Books Ltd
32-34 Gordon House Road,
London NW5 1LP

Reprinted 1997 and 1998

A catalogue record of this book can be obtained from the British Library

ISBN 1 85375-206-1

Cover design by Andrea Purdie
Cover image A Japanese Samurai
by permission of Werner Forman Archive

Printed and bound in Great Britain by
Creative Print & Design Ltd., Wales

For Michelle Mullen,
My past, My present, My future

Contents

• Jiu-Jitsu • Judo • Aikido •

• Other Forms of Japanese Martial Arts •

CONTENTS

• *Martial Arts of the World* •

• *Weapons of the Martial Artist* •

Introduction

Fighting is as old as man himself. This struggle to overcome another by means of combat, unarmed or armed, is perhaps the legacy handed down to us from our ancestors, the cave dwellers. Man has formulated scientific principles through the ages in his efforts to subdue enemies by fair means or foul. This quest for domination sowed the seeds for a fighting art.

The term 'martial arts' simply means arts concerned with the waging of war. Many of the martial arts we know today were developed from ancient war skills. In time, man's search for a deeper meaning to life, led to the development of a higher level of fighting. Ultimately, the old martial ways were used to cultivate man's understanding of himself.

This paradox of beginning as the practitioner of a lethal skill and along the way transcending the violent aims of that skill to become a human being with superior qualities in both mind and body, is perhaps best summed up by the Chinese proverb: 'He who overcomes others is strong. He who overcomes himself is mighty'.

The martial arts of the Orient are shrouded in mystery

and tradition. Each country seems to have developed its own fighting skills and through trial and error, honed them to perfection. Although many of these fighting arts differ tremendously from one another, there is one constant throughout – that is the almost pathological urge for anonymity. It is because of this brotherhood of secrecy that many of the martial arts we know today have only come to light within the last 50 years or so.

Many martial arts of the East have their roots buried deeply in religion. *Taoism* and *Buddhism* and their many offshoots have all played important roles in the development of fighting systems. The servants of these religious disciplines, the monks and priests, were for the most part responsible for spreading the various fighting skills all over Asia.

In the Middle East, murals in tombs in the Nile Valley and hieroglyphics engraved in the pyramids prove that the Egyptians had an organized type of unarmed combat as early as 3500 BC. For more complete information on a systematized martial method of fighting we must also look to the ancient Greeks. The works of the poet Homer (8th century BC) contained graphic descriptions of unarmed combat, and the philosopher Plato (428-348 BC) mentions in his writings a kind of shadow boxing termed *skiamachia*. This was eventually combined with the Greek system of wrestling to form an art called *pancration* meaning 'game of all powers'. In this system a wide variety of techniques was allowed. So far as is known, pancration was the first recorded fighting discipline that incorporated a method of kicking with punches and empty hand strikes. The art was eventually introduced, as a sport, into the Olympic Games in 648 BC.

Some historians believe that we should regard Alexander the Great (356-323 BC) as the founder of martial arts, bringing, through his invasion of India, the unarmed combat method of the Greeks to the East. However, it would seem somewhat naive to suppose that Asia had to wait for this Macedonian conqueror to invade her borders before the martial arts were born. Recent archaeological investigation in southern China has unearthed sketches and artefacts that suggest unarmed fighting methods were in operation long before his time.

Combat is identified with fighting and killing and yet, through the practice of martial disciplines, exponents have found increased spiritual awareness. Thus a strange paradox begins to emerge: a concept of inner peace beyond fighting. Ultimately, through continued studies, a search for a higher understanding of one's self is fostered. No one can train in a martial art discipline without at some stage becoming aware of this fundamental theme. To realize this, is to be half way towards grasping the true martial arts.

Karate

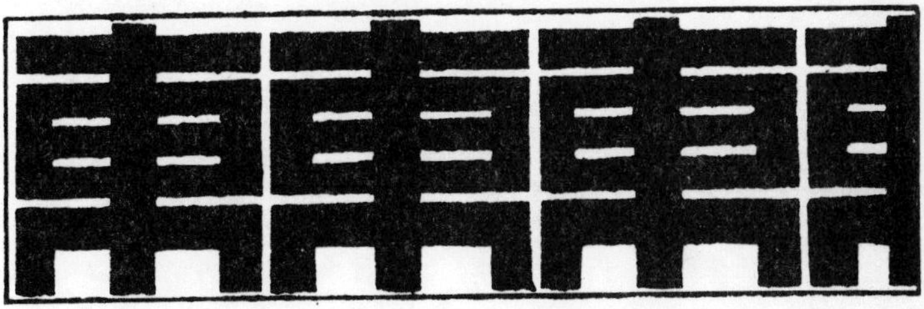

Karate

A gem is not polished without rubbing nor a man perfected without trials.

Origins of Karate

Karate literally means 'empty hand', although the correct term is *karate-do*, or 'way of the empty hand'. Karate comes from Okinawa, one of the Ryukyu Islands that form a chain of stepping stones between Japan and China. Because of their geographical position, it was there that the cultures of Japan and China met and fermented. In 1609, the island of Okinawa was invaded by Japanese troops. To prevent insurrection, the ruler of the island was taken back to Japan as a hostage and the Japanese quickly set up a police force in the capital, Naha to superintend internal affairs. Their next step was to ban the military class and confiscate all arms. The Japanese were confident that, without weapons, the Ryukyu islanders could not rebel.

But the invaders had not reckoned with the ancestral heritage of this island race – that of their martial arts. Because of Okinawa's close trade ties with China. The kung fu styles and methods of the latter country had mixed with the islanders' indigenous fighting arts.

Those unarmed arts were known as Okinawa *te*, which means 'hand'. The Ryukyu islanders, after consulting the old monks in the mountains, began to toughen their knuckles and elbows on straw pads and wet sand. Graduating to tree trunks, they pounded their fists into the trees day after day until eventually huge calluses built up on various parts of their bodies.

The armour of Japanese troops and even of the samurai, was made from lacquered bamboo and leather thongs. So when the Okinawans decided the time had come to fight back in guerrilla attacks, their deadly hardened fingers easily penetrated the armour of their oppressors, killing them instantly. When the Japanese sent mounted troops to quell the outbreaks of rebellion, the islanders devised a series of lethal kicks, executed while flying through the air. So even a mounted enemy proved to be no obstacle. The farmers played their part in fighting back by transforming agricultural implements into deadly weapons. The handle of a rice grinder, called a *tonfa,* was used to parry the blows from a samurai sword. The sickle for cutting the crops, known as a *kama,* made an excellent weapon against spear and sword attacks.

It was the transformation of these farming implements that today has given rise in the martial arts to Okinawan *kobudo* – the study of the classical weaponry of Okinawa.

The Birth of Modern Karate

Gradually, the Okinawans grew resigned to the fact that their Japanese overlords were going to stay forever. So they accepted the occupation with distaste but allegiance. In 1868 a man was born and named Gichin Funakoshi, the son of a minor official on Okinawa. The young Funakoshi grew up learning the martial skills of Okinawan te from a great master named Azato. By the time he was 25, Gichin Funakoshi had mastered the art and had also become a school teacher. When a visiting schools commissioner witnessed a demonstration of his art, Gichin Funakoshi was authorized to put martial arts on the educational curriculum. Karate had at last come out into the open, and was to be taught in schools throughout Okinawa.

Japan's introduction to what is now known as karate had to wait until 1912. It was then that the Imperial Navy's fleet, under Admiral Dewa, anchored in Chujo Bay, Okinawa. The ship's crews were housed in the school where Gichin Funakoshi taught, and the schoolmaster often put on impromptu demonstrations of karate for them. It was through this that karate came to be talked about in Tokyo. Nearly 10 years later, in 1921, the Emperor of Japan asked Funakoshi to perform his art in front of him. So impressed was the emperor at this exhibition of fighting skill, that he asked Funakoshi to travel to Japan and teach his art there. Within five years the mild-mannered Okinawan school teacher had become the idol of Japanese martial arts circles. By now Gichin Funakoshi was approaching his 60th birthday. He set up his first training school, or *dojo,* in Tokyo. It was known as *shotokan,* or the 'club of Shoto'. Funakoshi had previously used the pen-name of Shoto when he used to write poetry, so he felt that this name was quite appropriate. *Shoto* means 'waving pines'. Gichin Funakoshi had laid down the foundation for the biggest school of karate in the world. Although at that time his art was still known as Okinawan hand, it was later changed in Japanese calligraphy to its present name *karate-do* or 'the way of the empty hand'.

The influence of Funakoshi's new karate caused a rapid increase of karate schools in Japan as other masters from Okinawa went over to teach their own particular styles. Hot on the heels of Funakoshi was Chojun Miyagi of the goju-ryu school, and Kenwa Mabuni of the shito-ryu school. Many others came after them and pioneered the development of wado-ryu, shotokai, kyokushinkai, and shukokai. Today millions of karate practitioners all over the world practise any one of the 15 major styles and their many offshoots.

What is Karate?

Even in early training, the skills of a karate student are lethal because it is an all-in fighting system where everything is allowed. The concept of the art is to use every means available to the practitioner, and to overcome by technique, conditioning, and training an assailant or assailants in a fight for life. Karate is based on blows delivered with the hand, foot, head or knee. When he has mastered all these effective techniques, the student is awarded his first degree black belt, known as *shodan*, and he himself is then regarded as a *sensei*, or 'teacher'.

Originally, perhaps, the student takes up the art as an effective self-defence system. Then, as a result of hard training and the battle between mind and body to achieve instantaneous automatic reaction to any given situation, a feeling of inner calm and peace is experienced. The student reaches the point where he has won the fight within himself, and no longer needs to prove that he can fight. In fact, he will often prefer to walk away from trouble. But should that trouble follow him, he will be more than able to deal with it with deadly efficiency.

Karate Training

The hall or area where a student trains is called the *dojo*. The basic techniques are usually practised with a partner and then repeated over and over again. The only forbidden act in karate is to injure a training partner or a competition opponent. Ensuring this demands great skill and judgement. Part of the training is also centred on exercises performed against an imaginary opponent. This is called *kata*, and is very similar to shadow boxing. For many traditionalists this is the single most important aspect of karate. Many exponents of the art spend a whole lifetime just perfecting the movements and mental awareness of kata.

The Karate Kiai

A student must become familiar with all the vital areas of the body, and be able to focus a punch or kick on them at any given moment. To aid him during the performance of an impact technique, a *karateka*, one who studies karate, will emit a bloodcurdling shout known as the *kiai*. This kiai is brought up from the very depths of the lungs and emitted through the mouth as a shout, much as a weight-lifter shouts loudly before a heavy lift.

The kiai does two things. First, it brings a surge of power to a given blow, and second, when confronted with an emergency, this devastating shout from the lips of the intended victim just before he counter-attacks can momentarily confuse the assailant. It will at least put him off guard for those important few seconds before the karateka deals his blow.

Tamashiwara

In karate, as in other martial arts, there is a section called power-breaking or *tamashiwara*. In this, the student is called upon to break various hard materials by means of a blow from the fist, head, elbow, or even the fingertips. This power-breaking was originally intended to make the karate student aware of the tremendous power within himself. Today, however, the changing face of the art involve competition between the various martial arts power breakers to see who can break the most objects or the thickest wood.

The world record for breaking roofing tiles is held by the Japanese master, Masatatsu Oyama, who broke 30 tiles with one blow of his clenched fist.

At karate tournaments you will always see at least one demonstration of a tamashiwara expert driving his fist, knife hand (the edge of the hand), elbow, or head through anything from concrete to solid ice. Obviously a high degree of skill and training are necessary before a karateka can attempt such feats.

Mind over Matter

The mind and its powers plays a very important role in the makeup of a good karateka. Many strange stories have emanated from the training halls of Japan over the years. They tell of the great masters performing seemingly impossible feats of endurance, thanks mainly to their finely attuned mental powers. There are stories such as those of feeble old men breaking wood four and five inches thick, with gnarled and withered hands. But there is also the true story of one of karate's greatest heroes, who fought wild bulls with his bare hands. Before he retired he had fought nearly 50 bulls and killed at least three of them with his bare hands.

Richard Kim, a world renowned karate sensei was imprisoned in Manchuria by the Russians at the end of World War II. His captors did not like the way Kim seemed undisturbed by his captivity, so in an effort to make an example of him to the other prisoners they placed him in a cage with two tigers. The next morning the Manchurian guards found the tigers dead, with Kim sitting cross-legged in a relaxed pose. The man had no weapons in his possession, so how had he killed the tigers?

Another story tells of the famous goju-ryu sensei, Gogen Yamaguchi, whose nickname was 'The Cat', because he moved so swiftly. He was said to meditate under the full force of a waterfall every morning, and enjoyed the best of health all his life, when other mortals would almost certainly have died of pneumonia.

Scientists have often said that the power of the mind knows no boundaries. This certainly seems to be the case where the martial arts are concerned.

The Karate Dojo

The dojo is the hall where a karateka practises his art. Upon entering, he must bow from the waist. A great deal of respect and reverence must be shown while training in the dojo. When a student addresses the sensei, he bows before speaking. Strict behaviour is enforced and must be adhered to at all times. The students' karate suits are known as *gi,* and must be clean and well pressed. The karate uniform traditionally dates back to that of a simple Japanese peasant's garb. Which was a loose-fitting two-piece affair with wide baggy trousers.

The suit is held together with a very long belt, usually

coloured. The colour denotes the varying degrees of proficiency of its wearer. An absolute beginner is a white belt. According to the old traditions, when the white belt student passed his first grading exam he was awarded his *kyu* grade – this meant he was entitled to wear a different coloured belt. The student would then dye the belt the appropriate colour as he progressed through the kyu grades towards his black belt. The colours of the kyu grades becomes progressively darker with increased proficiency, thus enabling a student to keep the same belt throughout his training, just by dying it.

A karate dojo can be centred almost anywhere a sensei wants to teach his art.

Karate Belt Rankings

Regardless of the style and school of karate a practitioner comes from, all students have one goal in mind: to reach the standard of black belt. This can take anything up to five years to achieve. Once attained, the training does not cease; in fact, it becomes even more arduous. The black belt trains in the physical and mental disciplines of the art in an effort to reach the next class of grading. This is called a *dan*. After his second dan, the student will try even harder for his third dan, and so on.

This black belt dan ranking system comes from Japan, where it is used for virtually everything from swimming to *go*, a board game not unlike checkers.

The highest ranked Japanese black belt was Gogen Yamaguchi, who was ranked at tenth dan. Oddly enough, after ninth dan the colour reverts to red, which is the colour of a beginner's belt before he takes his first kyu examination. This symbolizes the fact that when one knows all, he returns to knowing nothing, yet understands everything.

Today, martial arts teachers all over the world have broken away from their traditional teachings and formed their own systems and styles. Because of this they can award themselves any high dan grade they wish. Therefore it is not uncommon to find teachers with sixth and seventh dan black belts at comparatively young ages.

The Karate Stance

The blows in traditional karate are delivered from a number of stances, each of which is suited to a particular purpose or situation. Certain styles of karate, such as goju-ryu, place much emphasis on the stance. When a student has undergone extensive training in stance work, he is put to the test by having planks of wood and long wooden poles broken on his body. Although this does seem to be somewhat masochistic, it does prove to the student what tremendous power he has within himself.

In Japan, a similar test is conducted, but minus the wooden planks. All students who are thought to be ready, line up in the straddle leg stance. The instructor walks up and violently kicks each one of them in the groin. Those that are left standing after this assault are deemed worthy of further advanced training.

Major Schools and Styles of Karate

Shotokan

This style of karate, founded by Gichin Funakoshi, is characterized by deep stances and powerful extended movements. It has numerous *kata*, or forms, which are practised with maximum strength. Funakoshi regarded the kata as the ultimate expression of his art, and devised many of them himself. The style uses considerable muscle power in the delivery of its techniques which are linear in their application.

Of the many great shotokan stylists Hirokazu Kanazawa stands out as perhaps one of the most skilful fighters of all time. In 1957 at the first All Japan Karate Championships he won every fight, including the final, with a broken hand - usually delivering the decisive blow with that hand. He accomplished this without ever having formally trained in free sparring for competition. The following year he won the championships again, only this time he also took the kata section. In recent years Kanazawa embarked on a serious study of tai chi chuan, to improve his health and extend his knowledge of the internal systems of the martial arts.

Kyokushinkai

This style was created by Masatatsu Oyama, who was once a student of shotokan under Funakoshi. Oyama was born in Korea, and was influenced by Chinese and Korean martial arts before he trained in shotokan. Not particularly impressed with the combat side of Funakoshi's style, he retired to the mountains in Chiba, where for the next two years he lived the life of a recluse. During this self-inflicted isolation, through intensive training and searching, he formulated a new karate system that was based upon actual combat effectiveness. He named this new style *kyokushinkai* or 'style of the ultimate truth'. To prove how realistic his new concept was, Oyama went to a slaughter house to fight with bulls. It has been recorded that over a period of time he fought 50 bulls, killing three of them outright with combination striking techniques.

In the early 1970s Oyama introduced a type of competition called knockdown. He has stated that this is the only true test of a karateka's fighting ability. It allows full power strikes to the body and kicks to the head. The bout ends when one of the fighters is knocked to the ground. Kyokushinkai training is severe and requires a certain amount of conditioning. It has been classed as one of the toughest styles there is. Oyama never stuck rigidly to the traditional techniques of karate, and was known in the later years of his life to have looked outside his own martial art for superior methods of fighting.

Wado-ryu

Wado-ryu was created by Hidenori Otsuka, and its name means 'way of peace or harmony'. Otsuka was another of Gichin Funakoshi's senior students. He was born in 1892 and his childhood was spent in the study of *shindo yoshin ryu* jiu-jitsu. He became so accomplished in this art he was awarded the headmastership of the style.

He first began the study of karate at the age of 30 under Funakoshi. Ten years later he broke away to form his own style, but for a number of years it had no name. Then in 1940, at a martial arts festival, he was asked to register a name for his school, which he did, calling it wado.

Hidenori Otsuka drew heavily upon his knowledge of

jiu-jitsu and merged it with his karate to found his style. This amalgamation of the yielding principles of jiu-jitsu, the non-opposition to strength, with the traditional Okinawan karate techniques gave a softness to the style that is unique in Japanese karate. Otsuka's karate system has a tremendously fast style and it is thought by many to be the fastest of all. Otsuka taught that the physical techniques and movements within wado are the expression of one's mind, in fact a manifestation of a person's spirit. He acknowledged three vital elements in the study of karate: physical strength, spirit and heart.

As Otsuka's system developed he felt that the art should embrace an element of sport. To this end he invented *kumite,* a form of sparring. Prior to this, there was no fighting in wado, just kata training. Since World War II his style has spread throughout Europe and America.

He was awarded his tenth dan (black belt ranking) by the brother of the emperor of Japan, and subsequently became the oldest practising karateka in the world. On the 29 January 1982, just four months short of his 90th birthday, Hidenori Otsuka finally passed away.

The practice of wado-ryu karate employs very light and fast techniques, favouring evasion, rather than meeting brute force head on. The practitioner defends by using a series of deflecting movements for blocking, then quickly counter-attacking as soon as an opening occurs. Twisting of the hips for increased power is also emphasized in this style. The basic stance is higher than it is in shotokan, enhancing speed and mobility. Students are taught to punch by creating a very fast type of whiplash movement. After delivery of a technique, the hand or foot is snapped back sharply to avoid capture by the opponent.

Because the style is competition oriented, a large amount of success has been accorded to its tournament practitioners in the world arena. In the late seventies wado-ryu in Europe splintered into a number of different associations, but undoubtedly its leading instructor is Tatsuo Suzuki, who now resides in London.

Goju-ryu

Goju-ryu, which means 'hard-soft style', was created by an Okinawan named Chojun Miyagi. Goju is one of the four major karate styles developed from the Okinawan art of *naha-te*, and its basis is the Yin and Yang principle of soft and hard.

Chojun Miyagi began training in naha-te at the age of 14 under the renowned instructor Kanryo Higaonna. As a youth Higaonna had made several trips to mainland China to learn Chinese boxing. Upon his return he merged his ideas with those of the indigenous karate systems of Okinawa. Two of his top students were Chojun Miyagi and Kenwa Mabuni.

After his master's death, Miyagi decided that he too would journey to the Chinese mainland to continue his studies. While there, he was greatly influenced by the subtleties of the Chinese internal systems of kung fu. Returning home to Okinawa a few years later he quickly established himself as a karate teacher par excellence.

Following the introduction of Funakoshi's karate to Japan, Okinawan teachers were in great demand. In 1928 Miyagi accepted a position as a karate instructor at Kyoto university, but Japan never really appealed to him. After bouts of homesickness he returned to Okinawa, only visiting Japan for limited periods from then on.

Chojun Miyagi devoted his whole life to the furtherance of goju karate. He died on 8 October 1953 aged 65. During his lifetime he saw his style remain pure, following the traditional patterns he had formulated, unlike the other karate styles which were splintering. While Miyagi was in Japan, he taught a student named Gogen

Yamaguchi. This student was to make a name for himself as the head of an off-shoot of goju, called goju-kai.

Goju-kai

After a visit to Shanghai Chojun Miyagi began to modify his karate system even further. A one time student of his, Gogen Yamaguchi, refused to accept the adjustments, believing that the old ways were the best. Thus he broke away to form his own style called goju-kai. Yamaguchi, known in karate circles around the world as 'The Cat', developed goju in Japan until it received the recognition that it has today. Because Miyagi refused to stay for long periods of time in Japan, it was left to Yamaguchi to popularize his own system. When Yamaguchi realized just how important he had become in Japanese karate circles, he took his responsibilities in earnest. For a time he went into the mountains to seek spiritual guidance from a group of Shinto priests. Once a wild man of karate, he now began a hard training regimen and would meditate for long periods, going without food or drink, sometimes standing for hours under icy cold mountain waterfalls in the classical stance of goju called *sanchin* meaning 'hourglass'.

During World War II he was captured by the Russian troops and shipped off to a labour camp in Mongolia. It was here, despite terrible hardship and deprivation, that Yamaguchi's karate spirit enabled him to survive. Nearly a year later he was repatriated, and in 1948 he opened his first dojo in Japan. Two years later he established the All Japan Karate-do Goju-kai.

The techniques in goju centre around close-quarter fighting. This highly complex style is quite exacting, requiring a balance between hard and soft, with the ability to change techniques in a quickly flowing, strong manner. The traditions of the school are maintained through training methods which are not just based on muscular strength – a great deal of emphasis is placed upon special breathing techniques. A beginner must master these correctly to attain any worthwhile standard. In the original style there were no high kicks although today with the advent of sport karate some are now used. Traditionally, high kicks to the head were not employed because they were considered unsafe, with the line of balance too exaggerated.

Gogen Yamaguchi's thoughts on a lifetime spent in karate can be best summed up in his answer to the question: What is karate all about ? He replied: 'Karate is not about fighting; it is about truth. The karate I teach cannot be understood without studying the Shinto religion and exploring yoga and then applying this knowledge to the art of karate itself'.

Shito-ryu

Shito-ryu karate was created by Kenwa Mabuni, an Okinawan. He had studied under the same master as Funakoshi. Mabuni had two teachers, Itosu and Higaonna, and it is after these two instructors that Mabuni named his style. The word comes from the Japanese characters used to write his teachers' names. Following in Funakoshi's footsteps, Mabuni began teaching karate in Japan, opening his first club in Osaka in 1934. Mabuni had a particular penchant for the practice of kata, and began to assimilate as many as possible, taking katas from the schools of shotokan, goju and shorin-ryu. In all there are more than 60 different katas, including those employing weapons.

Shukokai

One of Mabuni's senior students, Chojiro Tani, split from the association to develop his own theories on karate aimed at tournament fighting, which was becoming increasingly popular. Chojiro Tani named his new style *shukokai* meaning 'way for all'. Tani's innovative research and experimentation led to higher stances, faster kicks and direct blocks. The style was developed for speed and, because of the shorter stances, promoted good mobility. The delivery of attack appears to take importance over everything else. Shukokai techniques emphasize relaxation before the impact of a punch, thereby increasing acceleration and creating a greater force. It was to this end that foam punching pads were introduced as training aids. Karate students can hit the pad which is held by the training partner and actually feel the power being generated, rather than spend weeks punching into thin air. In the early days of shukokai, students believed wholeheartedly in the one blow punch, and would never put two or three together; the idea was that if you needed three punches, then you were not putting everything into the first one. However, when the style became influenced by the West, where practitioners wanted to be entertained as well as taught, and with the advent of sporting tournaments the number of kicks and punches within the Shukokai curriculum were expanded and combinations became the order of the day.

The basic stance of the style is simply that of a person walking. The mechanical movements practised in some of the other karate schools in Japan were strictly discouraged, the emphasis being placed on naturalness and relaxed use of the limbs. To avoid tension within the muscle groups, the system emphasized open hand techniques. The reasoning behind this is that if students clench their fists they will instinctively want to squeeze, thus tightening their muscles. The open hand also allows a very flexible wrist action, giving increased acceleration for punching or blocking.

The Western Concept

Even today it can be seen that the eastern methods of fighting are still undergoing a constant evolution. Scientific research in the West into the furtherance of athletic endurance and nutritional combinations for prolonged performances are perhaps taking the practice of traditional karate away from its early traditions, by placing too much emphasis on peak performance rather than the spiritual awareness and mental aims of the art. The most vital ingredient in the practice of successful karate is the power of the mind, but one wonders if, with the harnessing of western science, these time-tested arts are losing their true direction.

Kung Fu

Kung Fu

To ask is a moment's shame, not to ask and remain ignorant, is a lifelong shame.

Origins of Kung Fu

In the previous chapter we saw how karate was exported to Japan from Okinawa, where it grew and developed. There are various theories as to where the martial arts, as we know them today, came from. It is generally accepted that the birthplace of kung fu was in northern China around 520 AD. Recent findings offer the distinct possibility that a primitive martial art form reached the East via the Fertile Crescent in Mesopotamia, to be later developed in India and China. Or possibly much earlier: for instance, there is a Babylonian plaque held in the British Museum dating back 5,000 years or more, which depicts figures using systematized blocking and countering techniques.

The Wandering Monk

Most of the kung fu practised today is said to have originated in the Shaolin Monastery on Songshan Mountain, Honan province, in northern China.

It was introduced there by a wandering Indian monk

name Bodhidharma, also known as Ta-Mo. Bodhidharma was the son of King Sugundha of India. As befitted the son of royalty, in his youth Bodhidharma was well versed in the martial arts of his homeland, and was a much respected member of a warrior caste. In his middle years Bodhidharma for some reason now lost to us renounced his birthright, took up the robes of priesthood and set off on a life in pursuit of truth and knowledge. History records that some years later Bodhidharma surfaced in Honan province, having crossed the seemingly impenetrable barrier of the Himalayas on foot. He came to a monastery named Shaolin where he found the monks in an emaciated state. According to legend, Bodhidharma introduced the monks to a series of exercises in an effort to get them fit and well. The 18 exercises he taught them were for conditioning the body and developing the mind. These therapeutic movements are popularly believed to be the forerunners of Shaolin temple boxing, known as the 'Eighteen Hands of Lo-Han'.

Bodhidharma also brought Buddhist teaching and philosophies to these monks. It is believed that the Shaolin temple was the birthplace of the Ch'an philosophies, popularly known in the West as Zen.

The System Expanded

For 500 years or more, the Shaolin monks of Honan were feared as extraordinary fighters. They were men who, if they had to, could kill with their bare hands, although they upheld the Buddhist reverence for all forms of life. The only exception to this was in a life or death situation, when it was kill or be killed.

In 1589 a man named Kwok Yuen entered the temple and expanded Bodhidharma's 18 exercises to 72. To increase the number of fighting systems Kwok Yuen disguised himself as an old man and wandered around the country in search of skilled teachers of kung fu. Upon his return to the temple with new instructors, the Shaolin boxing system was expanded even further, bringing the number of movements up to 170. These were then classified into five distinct styles: tiger, crane, leopard, snake, and dragon. Later, these individual styles were improved into a more effective system known as the 'five animals fist'.

The Test of Courage

Whenever a young monk undergoing training at Shaolin was thought ready to leave, having mastered all the skills of kung fu, he had to take a life-or-death test. According to legend there were only two doors to the temple: the side door, which gave exit from and entry to the grounds, and the main entrance, which was only used by masters upon leaving. The candidate, in order to prove that he was a master of kung fu, had to make his way to this exit via a specially designed labyrinth filled with all manner of traps and dangerous obstacles designed to test his skills to the utmost. If the candidate failed the test, he would die in the tunnels and never be heard of again. The successful candidate, having mastered all the perils of the labyrinth, would eventually emerge at the front gate only to find it blocked by a huge smouldering metal urn. He had to move his last obstacle before gaining his freedom.

Because of its weight, the monk would have to bare his forearms and grasp the urn in his arms to lift it out of the way. In doing so, the front gate would be triggered open. Each side of the urn had a dragon carved on it. As the monk lifted this obstacle, he would be branded by the red-hot metal with the mark of the dragons on his forearms. This signified to everyone that the man marked with the twin dragons was a fighting priest of Shaolin, and a master of kung fu.

The Shaolin Temple

The Shaolin temple in Honan was not the only temple where kung fu was practised. In fact, there were numerous temples in and around China named Shaolin, and most of them had thriving kung fu classes.

Though the two religions of Taoism and Buddhism were equally popular, Shaolin was strictly Buddhist. The Taoist temple was named Wa Lum, and was located in Shantung. The name Sil Lum is Cantonese for Shaolin, and not another monastery, as some people believe.

The five ancestors generally regarded as the founders of the present-day Triad societies were survivors of the Shaolin temple after it had been burnt and sacked by the Ching emperor K'sing-Hsi in 1674. Although the monks had often used their fighting skills on the battlefield in support of the emperor, plotting at court persuaded him that they posed a threat to the throne and should be disbanded. A huge army was mustered and, so legend has it, with the help of a renegade Shaolin monk, the temple was attacked and razed to the ground. Out of the 118 resident monks, 100 perished in the flames. The 18 survivors fled, but 13 of them were caught and killed. The remaining five managed to cross the Yellow River and escape.

Legacy of the Ancients

Much of what was learned about the martial arts was handed down by word of mouth only and was shrouded in myth and secrecy. The ancient masters did not reveal their knowledge readily. Only students who were truly dedicated were allowed to glimpse into the techniques of the particular style that the master was teaching, and this was only after their sincerity and absolute devotion to the art had been thoroughly tested.

Through a long series of both difficult and menial tasks the master would ascertain how seriously the budding devotee intended to study his school's particular style of martial art. This early form of character analysis worked very well indeed, and rarely was a master ever let down by a student he had tested. Even today in certain schools of martial arts, this age-old system for accepting only really dedicated students is still practised. Students have often waited years before being allowed the honour to train in even the most basic of techniques. Once accepted, they were bound to a code of secrecy and silence, and were forbidden to share with outsiders the wisdom and knowledge gained from their martial arts training.

Additionally, because of the political intrigue in China, and constant power struggles between the generals and court politicians, practice of the martial arts was often concealed from the authorities, and daily training was carried out behind the confines of the temple walls.

When the head of a martial system knew that either through old age or illness his years were numbered, a search would begin among the senior students for a successor to carry on the style after the master's death. The advanced techniques would then be taught to that chosen person, so that the finer points could be perpetuated. If it should happen that the chosen disciple did not meet the master's requirements, the all important central core would be withheld and would die with the master, leaving behind only a shallow outline of a once great system.

The Principles of Kung Fu

To achieve the slightest understanding of kung fu, a person has to be familiar with the underlying principles and constant theme of the Chinese martial arts. Most methods of kung fu appear to encompass philosophies based on nature, religion, and cosmology. Fighting techniques have been adapted from mammals, birds, insects, and even patterns of tidal flow. A symbol that is seen inside kung fu *kwoons*, or schools, all over the world is the *Yin-Yang*. This famous symbol, surrounded by eight trigrams, figuratively expresses nature and its changes. It is also known as the double fish symbol, representing opposites residing together. In the heart of Yin, the negative force of cold, darkness, and emptiness, is a tiny part of Yang – which is warmth, light, and positive energy. And in the heart of Yang is a small part of Yin.

This indicates that within strength is found weakness; within hardness, softness; and activity within inactivity. These alternating forces are indestructible and inexhaustible. They contradict as well as complement each other. The Chinese believe that without understanding this eternal duality one can never comprehend the true essence of kung fu, or the power that regulates the very universe itself.

The Two Basic Schools of Kung Fu

Chinese martial arts are generally divided into two broad approaches: one is the internal or soft school, and the other is the external or hard school. The internal encompasses the martial arts of *pa-kua*, *hsing-i*, and *tai chi chuan*. These Chinese boxing arts put the stress on the metaphysical and philosophical aspects of the art. The external systems are associated with Shaolin *chuan-fa* meaning 'Shaolin fist', *hung gar*, and *tong long*. These schools stress power strikes, hand and body conditioning, and utilize force in straight lines, with much greater emphasis on kicking.

The internal schools are usually considered to be defensive and passive, whereas the external systems are often more aggressive and muscular in approach.

A recurring influence throughout the oriental martial arts is that of religion. Many of the martial arts are closely related to either Buddhism or Taoism, both of which believe in attaining salvation through the cultivation of harmony in mind and body.

Chinese boxing, or kung fu, evolved into five major styles named by their creators – Hung, Lau, Monk, Choy, and Li. The many changes that these styles have gone through over the ages have resulted in the kung fu schools that we know today.

The Family System

The study and practice of kung fu in China built strong schools that were bound together like a family structure. The *sifu*, teacher, resembled the father figure, and the *sihings*, advanced students, were looked upon as older brothers. The novices and beginners were classed as younger brothers. Everyone in the school worked under a system based on self-discipline and sacrifice to perfect his art to the best of his ability. It is through this dedication and training that the arts of kung fu have survived the turbulent history of ancient China, to become a significant and vital aspect of today's martial arts.

The External or Hard Schools of Kung Fu

From the legacy handed down by the Shaolin monastery, many styles of kung fu have developed and the original five animals have been expanded many times over.

At a conservative estimate, there are about 1500 distinct kung fu styles practised today, although many are still guarded with secrecy on mainland China.

It is only during the past 10 years or so that Chinese teachers have come out into the open and taught westerners their art. At one time only Chinese would be accepted into the student ranks. They were known as 'closed door students'. In the early 1960s, a westerner had to be something very special to warrant instruction from a Chinese master.

All of the kung fu styles combined undoubtedly hold the key to every possible defensive and offensive movement within their systems. Because it takes many years to complete just one of those systems, nobody can know everything. As a result each practitioner of kung fu always believes his systems to be the best, and that as such it can beat all others. This gave rise to much in-fighting between rival schools. And even today in Hong Kong there are at least two or three bouts of *kong sau*, 'secret fighting', every week in an effort to gain supremacy over a rival school of kung fu.

All the kung fu systems have their special merits, but there is no one system that is superior to all the rest. Many masters have come up with special movements based on all manner of fauna, but they still contain potential flaws or restrictions.

Hung Gar Chuan

Of the external styles, one of the most popular is hung gar chuan. *Hung* is the name of the originator, *gar* means 'family', and *chuan* means 'fist'. This is a southern Chinese style and was adapted from the Shaolin tiger system. It incorporates the white crane style and emphasizes very low, strong stances. Novices are supposed to stand in the *ma-pu,* or so called 'horse stance' practising punching for three hours every day for three years before they are allowed to continue with further techniques. The system is said to possess a thrust punch that always results in a knockout.

Hung gar is characterized by internal power and low wide stances that produce strong solid legs. The movement in hung gar is direct and generally close to the body, but when a strike connects with an opponent, it can show considerable force. The strong low stance is also noticeable in other kung fu styles, but perhaps none emphasizes it as much as hung gar.

The style's low stance reputedly came from Hung's secret training sessions on board Chinese junks while he was a rebel and on the run from the Manchus. These junks had very low roofs and bobbed about on the water constantly, so therefore to practise successfully on a regular basis, it was necessary to adapt the Shaolin styles, with their sweeping foot patterns, to suit the confined space.

Because of the initial focus on this very low stance and the concentration on breathing exercises, more stamina and will power are required to learn the hung gar basics than those of other styles.

Hung gar makes use of a blocking technique known as a pounding block, which is executed with a hammer fist. For a practitioner to apply this block meaningfully and correctly, he has to undergo a great deal of hand and arm conditioning.

Praying Mantis or Tong Long

Legend has it that a kung fu master named Wong Long went to the Shaolin temple to challenge the monks to a fight because he had heard that these monks were undefeatable. After receiving persistent challenges, the abbot sent out a novice monk to fight him. Within seconds, the novitiate monk had thrown Wong Long to the ground and decisively defeated him. Building himself up with superior techniques, Wong Long twice more went back to Shaolin to fight the monks, only to return each time bitterly defeated. Wong Long retired in seclusion to the mountains and one day while sitting under a tree, he watched a fight between a grasshopper and a praying mantis. Although the grasshopper was bigger and stronger, it could not overcome the smaller and weaker mantis. Eventually the grasshopper was beaten and devoured by the praying mantis. Highly impressed by what he had seen, Wong Long teased the mantis with a piece of long grass and memorised every defence and attack movement the mantis made. Wong Long proceeded to devise a fighting system based on the movements of that little praying mantis. Returning to Shaolin, he issued the same challenge yet again, and this time Wong Long defeated all comers.

The most distinctive movement in the mantis or tong long system is that of the mantis hand, which when attacking is shaped like a hook and looks like the insect's doubled-up forelegs. The fast footwork is based on the hops executed by the long-legged mantis.

The system employs two basic principles. The first is the grab. This is effected by shaping the hands to resemble that of a mantis's claw, with the index finger pointed forward. Grabbing is followed by pulling, to expose certain areas of the body. Then strikes are made to these vital points. Skilled pulling also ensures that the opponent is off balance. The second principle is what is known as 'monkey footwork' which does not, as the name implies, copy the footwork of a monkey, but rather imitates its speed and agility, while still giving support and balance. The stances are short, with a quick sideways stepping motion.

Although both northern and southern mantis schools use the name of praying mantis in their titles, the methods and fighting principles of the styles are quite different. Northern mantis stresses long range fighting tactics and also includes a wide variety of kicks. Southern mantis schools rely heavily upon fighting techniques delivered from close range with a more stable stance. Although kicks are seldom used, when they are, they are aimed at the groin or knee-caps.

Choy Lee Fut

In 1836 Chan Heung founded the system of kung fu called *choy lee fut*. The style was named after his two teachers Lee Yau-Shan and Choy Fook. *Fut* means 'Buddha' in Chinese. In his early years Chan fought against the British in the Opium Wars. He taught his kung fu to local villagers in the hopes of forming a militia but, beaten by the British after one of the many uprisings, he fled to Nanking. There he set up one of the many tong and triad societies that flourished at that time. In his later years he went to America, settling in San Francisco, where he opened a kung fu kwoon.

Chan Heung was born in King Mui village in Kwantung province (c.1802). From a very early age he was a student of hung gar kung fu. In his early twenties he decided to expand his knowledge of fighting styles, so he set out to search for a hermit named Choy Fook who lived somewhere in the mountains. This monk was famous throughout China as one of the greatest boxing masters of all time, but few people had been able to find him since his retirement. Chan Heung searched for many months until he eventually met up with him.

Chan Heung spent ten years with Choy, learning everything he could from his system. When Chan Heung was satisfied that he had mastered sufficient techniques, he left Choy Fook and retired in solitude for a number of years to refine all that the monk had taught him. He added to this his hung gar experience and the few years' training he had had previously with an another monk named Lee Yau-Shan. Then in 1836 Heung emerged with his own system, naming it after the two people who had given him the nucleus.

Many weapons are used in the style such as the tiger fork and double knives. Perhaps the most unusual is the 'nine dragon trident'. The head of this spear type of weapon has nine objects resembling hooks, thought to remind users of dragons' teeth. This weapon is so heavy that ordinary practitioners have trouble using it. The double knives of the system were short and had very heavy blades in order that one blow even if mis-aimed could cause devastating damage to an opponent. After the treaty of Nanking, the document that put an end to the Opium Wars in China leaving the British as the victors, many secret societies were formed and ritual killings between rival Triad societies became commonplace, and it was the double knives that were the favoured weapon of these killings.

Choy lee fut is one of the most popular kung fu styles in the world today. It is an all-purpose fighting art that uses grabbing and seizing methods. Punching is distinctive because of its long circular strikes, the blows being released only a foot away from the target. A student of this style attacks by running straight into an opponent and unleashing a whirlwind of overpowering hooks and uppercuts.

Wing Chun

Thanks to the late Bruce Lee, *wing chun* is probably the best known of all kung fu styles, because Lee looked to wing chun to form the nucleus of his own style of jeet kune-do. Wing chun originated some 400 years ago. It was founded by a nun named Yim Wing Chun. Her teacher, Ng Mui, was one of the few people to escape the sacking of Shaolin by the Ching troops, when they burnt the monastery to the ground. She and a few of the monks managed to seek refuge in Central China. Ng Mui was an instructor of *mui fa chuan* or 'plum flower fist'. In the village where she settled down Ng Mui met Yim Wing Chun as a young girl, and taught her the system. But Yim Wing Chun thought that the plum flower fist was too complex and placed too much reliance on power techniques and strong horse stances, befitting a man rather than a woman. Yim Wing Chun wanted something that was not complicated yet efficient, as a means for defending herself. Not finding it among existing styles, she created her own. She dedicated her style to the Buddhist nun who had taught her, but named it after herself. Wing chun means 'beautiful springtime'.

The art first came to light in the West when its modern instigator, grandmaster Yip Man, left the town of Fatshan on the Chinese mainland during the communist takeover to live in Hong Kong. Yip Man had one great desire, which was to make wing chun known all over the world. He had achieved much of his aim by 1972, when he died aged 78.

An adept of wing chun concentrates on defending his centre line. This is an imaginary line running through the centre of his body, where all the vital organs lie. The overall simplicity of wing chun is evident by the number of workable techniques involved in learning the system. There are only three forms to learn in order to gain mastery. Even the weapons system is limited to just two implements – the butterfly knives, and the six-and-a-half-point pole.

The Fighting Monkey

An unusual style of kung fu is that of the 'mischievous monkey', or to give it its correct name, *ta sheng pi' kua mern*. The system is in fact two styles combined.

Ta sheng was founded by Kou Sze during the early years of the Chinese Republic (1911-1949). He was already proficient in an obscure style of kung fu called *ti tang mern* or 'grand earth method', which specialized in ground fighting techniques and kicks. Kou Sze worked as a bodyguard, but because of the trouble and turmoil in the new republic he planned to give up his job and return home. On the way, while staying in a little village, he was arrested and accused of murdering another man during a fight. Kou Sze explained to the authorities that the death had occurred purely as a result of defending himself. Four men had attacked him as he was passing. He had beaten them off using his kung fu skills, but as a result one of them had died. The court believed his story and on these grounds spared him the death penalty, but he was still sentenced to eight years' imprisonment

During his prison years his cell window faced a hillside on which resided a colony of monkeys. Every day while practising his kung fu in the confines of his cell, he watched the monkeys playing and fighting. Kou Sze became fascinated by their speed and agility and in the way they seemed to make very crafty moves. By observing them closely he began to catalogue their many and varied movements. Later he adapted these monkey antics into his own training regimen. By the end of his sentence, Kou Sze had perfected his new style.

Upon leaving prison, Kou Sze went to see his friend who was a master of Pi Kua Mern, but found he had died. The son offered to put him up for a time. Kou Sze told his friend's son about his new style and explained that he had named it *ta sheng* or 'great sage' in honour of the monkey king god. The son was impressed and took it upon himself to learn the complete system from Kou Sze.

When Kou Sze died some years later, the son merged his own style of pi kua mern.

The Drunken Monkey

Perhaps the most famous of all the monkey fighting techniques (known as sets) in the system is that of the 'drunken monkey'. This set is supposedly based upon the actions of a monkey that stole some wine and subsequently became drunk. The fighting techniques accredited to this form teach the student to stagger and lurch around as if drunk. This ploy baffles the opponent, sometimes amusing him, so the opponent catches his aggressor off guard and suddenly launches into a series of strong unsuspected attacks.

A student of this style has to adopt the mannerisms and behaviour of a monkey, to truly understand the principle behind the art. It is not uncommon to enter a kwoon and see students pulling faces, screeching and jumping up and down, in emulation of monkeys.

Other Styles

Within the range of Chinese fighting systems come all manner of weird and wonderful titles – 'drunken man boxing', 'the white eyebrow', *fu jow pai*, or 'tiger claw' – the list is endless. Even mythical animals such as the dragon and the unicorn have given their names to fighting styles. Today in Hong Kong there are certain kung fu systems that even now have never been taught to anyone who is not of pure Chinese blood.

The Internal or Soft Schools of Kung Fu

Of the three internal styles of kung fu practised today, *tai chi chuan* has the greatest following. It has been adopted by the West more for its exercise principles than for its combat methods.

In the 13th century in China, there lived a monk named Chang San Feng. Growing a little disinterested in the martial arts of the day, he retired to the mountains to seek wisdom and knowledge. One night Chang dreamt that God himself had taught him how to fight. The dream bothered the old monk and he spent many days pondering the meaning of it. Realization came as he watched a crane and a snake battling for supremacy. Neither could gain the advantage. Fascinated by the scene, the monk went on to study the techniques of these animals. When the crane attacked, the snake would outmanoeuvre the bird by twisting and turning. Likewise, when the snake attacked, the crane would lift its feet, flap its wings, and go perch on the limb of a tree.

Chang saw that, unlike external systems where an attack was met by equal force, this fighting concept of the strong becoming yielding and the yielding becoming the strong, was completely new. He came to understand that counting on superior power to defeat an opponent was not enough in itself, and was perhaps even contrary to the laws of nature.

Continued studies showed Chang that force begets force, and often the best way to overcome force was not to fight it at all. The premise behind his new 'soft style' was simply to maximize internal energy through tranquillity and thus minimize wasted external energy.

Tai Chi Chuan

Translated as the 'grand ultimate fist', *tai chi chuan* or *tai chi*, as it is commonly called, is a form of Chinese boxing, with all its movements based on self-defence, it is because of its health aspect that practitioners are adopting this style of kung fu. Tai chi is sometimes called moving meditation. It is steeped in philosophy and based on the principles of the Chinese classic, the *I-Ching* by Lao Tzu. The movements are continuous; there is no break from one to another and the practitioner is continually striving to push forward. The therapeutic benefits of the tai chi form affect young and old alike. So startling have been the health improvements after six months of training in tai chi that extensive research is being carried out to discover why this ancient Chinese combat form is benefiting millions of people all around the world. In the past few years research has shown that daily practice of the tai chi form combats stress and anxiety at every level. Some big companies have even gone so far as to send its executives to classes to help them minimize mental fatigue and stress.

The benefits of tai chi are spread right across the board. Old people from London to San Francisco have been given a new lease of life since taking up tai chi. It has even been reported by one tai chi group that a number of senior citizens enrolled in a class, the majority of whom were in wheelchairs. Within four months of learning the form, they had left their wheelchairs at home and were standing on their own without support, doing tai chi.

The Elixir of Life

Legend relates that tai chi was founded by Chang San Feng. Feng was a Taoist alchemist who lived in the mountains during the Yuan dynasty (1279-1368). After drinking a strange concoction one day, he fell into a deep sleep and had a dream in which he was taught a series of fighting manoeuvres all centring around completely yielding to an oncoming attack. He began to practise these each day and within two years his elderly frame began to grow strong and youthful. He believed that at last he had found the elixir of life.

Feng left the mountains to head for civilization and teach this new art to the people. In his journey through the wilderness it is said that on many occasions he was attacked by bandits who roamed the area and Feng defeated every one of them.

In later life Chang San Feng took a disciple under his wing named Chen Chia Kou and taught him everything about tai chi. The Chen family kept the secret of the form for over 400 years. Later on, Chen's descendants elaborated on the system and the style split into two branches. One member of the family was engaged by a druggist to teach his sons, and the servant of that family, Yang Lu-Chan watched and learnt the style in secret until he was finally accepted as a student. Yang later went to Peking and taught the emperor's guards his 'internal' boxing methods. As a result the famous Yang tai chi form was developed, which today is practised all over the world.

The dreamlike dance movements of the tai chi form are almost hypnotic. The exercise is performed quite literally in slow motion. It stresses tranquillity in the midst of movement. The idea is to become like water and flow, envelop, the object being to unite mind and body in a state of complete harmony.

Tai Chi in Combat

Tai chi makes use of stillness in movement to contain movement. In its combat form, you wait for the other person to move and then you harness their force. When you do tai chi you should be relaxed but not limp. This is softness on the outside but energy or hardness within, like an iron bar wrapped in cotton. The concept of defence in tai chi is really quite simple. The attacker attacks, and without moving, the defender absorbs his direct energy and then repulses it. This direct force hitting the assailant head-on send him sailing backwards through the air as far as 20 feet.

Because tai chi is the softest of the internal arts, the students of the hard styles of karate and kung fu seek it out to complement their own particular art. Many years are required to uncover the subtle secrets of tai chi. Once proper knowledge of the art is cultivated a practitioner will know how to ward off an on-coming attack and flow right into a counter-move. Warding off and counter-attacking are the key manoeuvres in tai chi and for this reason it is said to reflect best of all the philosophical premises of Yin and Yang.

Pa-kua

The I-Ching or 'Book of Changes' is reputed to be one of the oldest books in the world, dating back more than 3,000 years. The I-Ching has a dual role in Chinese thinking: it is an oracle or book of divination and also a manual of philosophical and moral doctrine. The book centres around the eight trigrams formalizing the interplay of yin and yang. These eight trigrams are combined into 64 hexagrams which are said to relate to the understanding of all things under heaven that are in nature.

Pa-kua, the second of the internal forms of kung fu, means 'eight trigrams', and like tai chi it is based on the I-Ching. The style is founded upon the premise that if you can defend yourself at the eight compass points covered by the trigrams you will be fully protected from attack. pa-kua has many open-palm techniques for striking, and the footwork is based on the circle. When an attack is made, the aggressor is likely to find that his victim has avoided his blow and has got around behind him in order to retaliate.

Walking the Circle

In the practice of pa-kua, the movements correspond with those original eight trigrams, and the emphasis is on turning in a circle with very few straight-line manoeuvres. Students begin by learning to 'walk the circle' this is an exercise for gaining mastery of pa-kua's unique stepping patterns. As in tai chi which has the one form with 128 movements, so pa-kua has one central pattern which is the foundation on which the rest of the art is built. This is called *da mu hsing* or 'great mother form'. Specific techniques are practised while walking this circle. The student's aim is to move around an opponent, constantly circling in an effort to find an opening in which to strike. This is the prime strategy. At later stages an internal energy is gradually developed, that of *chi*. This intrinsic power accumulates within the individual, and is perhaps one of the hardest qualities to understand, especially in the West where logic seems to rule and strength is identified with rippling muscles.

As the student develops his chi levels, the subtle body movements are totally relaxed. These involve spiralling and twisting. The spiralling is likened to a corkscrew, with the body spinning while moving up and down. The twisting is from the waist, with the aim of generating tremendous power. An exponent, when adept, can virtually turn his waist right around to its extremes, to promote a recoiling power that is quite exceptional.

The Mountain Priest

Comparatively speaking pa-kua is a newcomer to the martial arts, only coming to prominence in the last 200 years or so, although the concept of internal boxing goes back about 400 years or more. Pa-kua was brought to light mainly through the practices of its alleged founder Tung Hai-Chuan, who was a eunuch in the palace of the Ching emperor, Tao Kuang. Prior to this, not a lot is known about the early life of Tung. He was a native of Hopei province and he spent much of his time one step ahead of the law. During one brush with the authorities he escaped imprisonment by seeking refuge in a monastery, where he furthered his skills in Chinese boxing methods. But his constant bad behaviour and drunken ways led him to be expelled. After further adventures Tung headed for the mountains to become a bandit. It was here that he came upon an old Taoist hermit. He witnessed the remarkable sight of an aged man practising what appeared to be a boxing style, but nothing like the kung fu he himself had trained in, or for that matter had ever seen before. The old priest was twisting and spiralling up and down, walking backwards and forwards in a circle, constantly changing direction. The hermit executed these strange moves with all the grace and agility of a man 40 years his junior. Tung approached the monk for instruction in this mysterious art and spent the next 10 years perfecting his skills. The next we hear of Tung Hai-Chuan, he is in Peking, where he is acknowledged by all for his genius in kung fu.

Miraculous Feats

Many of Tung Hai-Chuan's miraculous feats have been recorded and handed down by way of myths and tales. One story describes Tung sleeping in a chair. A student noticing him, crept up to throw a blanket over him. The blanket landed, but Tung had vanished and was found at the opposite end of the room in another chair and still asleep.

It is generally accepted that Tung is the founder of pa-kua, but many martial arts historians disagree and claim that pa-kua has its origins almost 5,000 years ago, around 2953-2838 BC when the emperor Fu Hsi first used the term. Fu Hsi is supposed to have gained his inspiration for these eight trigrams from the deeply scarred markings on the back of a tortoise's shell. The trigrams were linked, according to Fu Hsi, with the five elements of earth, metal, water, wood and fire, which through Yin and Yang constituted the creative force of the universe, or the tao (way). The trigrams became incorporated into the I-Ching, as a means of foretelling the future.

Pa-kua, like the other internal styles has been mainly

influenced by Taoism, whereas the other Chinese systems of kung fu which were developed at Shaolin were mainly Buddhist.

One story relates how in 625 AD, some Taoist martial arts masters and their students met some Shaolin masters and students and together formed a pa-kua style known as *numin*. The head of this newly formed school was a master named Sun Fung Lee. *Nu* translated means 'a stream' and *min* is the old Chinese word for 'people'. It was quite literally a joining of two peoples into one particular stream of the martial arts.

In tai chi chuan there are the different styles such as yang, wu and chen. In pa-kua, numin is a style of the art; the art is the same, but with subtle, yet distinct differences as taught by various founding grandmasters.

Hsing-i

The third art of the internal systems is that of *hsing-i*, but this is at the opposite end of the scale to tai chi. It is the hardest of the three, that is in application rather than degree of difficulty. In contrast to pa-kua, hsing-i places great emphasis on linear movement. It works on the geometric principle that the shortest distance to an object is along a straight line and is similar in thinking to wing chun's centre line theory.

This theory of the straight line is incorporated into the practitioner's belief that he should never retreat but continue advancing head on. The style is characterized by forceful horizontal attacks with closed-fist punches.

Warrior Origins

Hsing-i was created in the 12th century by the Chinese warrior, General Yueh Fei, and stresses the complementary principle of yin and yang, of both hard and soft. The term hsing-i is derived from two words, *hsing* which means 'form', and *i* which denotes the mind or the will. Hsing-i is a physical manifestation of a philosophical premise. It reflects the Chinese belief that the yin and yang work through the five elements of wood, fire, water, earth and metal, each of which has the power to overcome another, while being subject to the power of yet another. Take for example fire, which is overcome by water, whereas water is overcome by earth, earth by wood and wood is conquered by metal which in turn is overcome by fire. The relationship between the martial arts and the theme of nature and the universe is constant.

In the art of hsing-i these elements are represented through the five basic movements, which are identified as splitting, crushing, pounding, drilling and crossing. Within this framework are the primary movements to cover all angles and direction of attack and defence. These basic motions have thousands of variations and are executed at very high speed. When the foundation of the five elements has been practised thoroughly, the student is then introduced to the first form called *lien hwan chuan*, which links these separately practised movements into a definite pattern of connected sequences.

Mind and Body Boxing

It is the aim of a hsing-i practitioner to unite the mind with the body, and this is perhaps why hsing-i is sometimes known as 'mind and body boxing'. There is very little wasted motion in the art; it is very direct in its application of short strikes. No tension is applied when punching, as the energy comes from within the body, rather than from muscular development. The physical techniques of hsing-i are not as important as the mental development; it is not so much a question of how much one does, but rather of how well one does it. Hsing-i stresses the development of chi energy whose internal power is channelled to make the hsing-i student's body like a piece of steel.

Finally students are taught what is known as the 'twelve animals'. These are a series of short forms supposedly derived from the characteristics of certain animals, for example, the bird, snake, tiger, horse and dragon. Although students go through the process of learning these forms, it is usual to find that true technical competence is demonstrated in only two or three of them, depending on the student's own capabilities. This is probably due to the differing sizes and physiques of the individuals learning them. Each animal has its own potential for a system of fighting. It is not necessary to learn the whole twelve animals before one becomes adept. The most commonly taught form in hsing-i is that of the tiger.

Legends of the Masters

In folklore the world over fanciful stories have emerged about heroes whose deeds defy the imagination. The annals of kung fu are rife with such tales. There was for example, the old monk named Hung Yun who lived in China during the Ming dynasty. In an effort to gain entrance to a certain monastery, he humbled himself by waiting outside the gates all day and all night in a raging blizzard. When he was brought in unconscious the next morning, drops of his blood fell on the earth outside. As the sun rose, the blood formed a red mist and floated across the sky. When his helpers saw this, they named him *Hung Yun*, meaning 'red cloud'. Hung later went on to found the tien shan pai system of kung fu, and his followers helped to stiffen Chinese resistance to the Manchurians and their Ching dynasty.

Then there is the story of the Tibetan lama who was disturbed while meditating by a lake. Turning around he saw a white crane and a huge ape locked in combat. It seemed almost certain that the crane would die as the ape gripped the bird with its massive paws, but the crane manoeuvred its body away from the ape's grip, and instead of fleeing, fought back with equal ferocity. Using its powerful wings for balance, it made repeated charged at the ape with its rapier-like beak poking at the vulnerable spots on the ape's body. Eventually the ape, after losing an eye fled to the shelter of the forest. The lama was so fascinated by what he had just witnessed that he went on to study the movements of the crane, and founded a kung fu system around it, naming the system for the crane.

Monks and holy men in kung fu folklore are always the central characters of the stories. This is because it was only those seekers of knowledge who had the time to formulate ideas. One old monk, who invented a very famous style of kung fu, was actually thrown out of the Shaolin temple. Bok Mei, as he was called, had a long white beard, long white hair, and huge eyebrows. While learning the skills of kung fu at Shaolin, he killed a fellow disciple. Because of this, even though it was an accident, he was expelled from the monastery with orders never to return. Bok Mei left and sought refuge in the mountains. As a result of his observations of nature, he created a style designed mainly for speed. It later became known as the 'white eyebrow style'. But Bok Mei's mistake was never forgotten at Shaolin and his style was banned by members of the Shaolin temple.

The Snake With No Legs

One old legend with a certain proverbial sting in the tale is that of 'painting legs on a snake'. There was once a great kung fu master who was in the autumn of his years and as tradition dictates, he had to hand down all the secret knowledge of his kung fu style to his most senior student. Seniority in this instance was dictated by more than just time served. The problem with this particular master was that he had two students of equal competence and skill. So in order to decide which one of the two students should inherit the secret learning and also become head man of the system, he set them a test. He ordered both students to go outside and each draw an animal in the dirt. The student who drew the animal the fastest and providing it was instantly recognizable by the master would inherit all.

Each student grabbing a stick, quickly set to work with the task. The first student's instinct was to quickly draw an elongated letter 'S' in the dirt; upon looking up he saw the second student still drawing away in the dirt. Feeling ill at ease because he had been too quick with the set task, he began to embellish upon his earlier attempt by adding a series of squiggles meant to represent legs. As he was about to add a third leg, the other student straightened up indicating he had finished the task. The master walked over and proclaimed the second student the winner and the true inheritor and heir apparent to the style. Turning to the first student, he asked 'Tell me, why did you carry on drawing after you had finished painting in the sand what was quite obviously a snake ?' The student replied, 'Because master, having thought of drawing a snake, and doing it so quickly I then had doubts that you would not recognize what it was supposed to be. So I had the bright idea to put legs on it, so that it would resemble a lizard'.

'The doubt in your mind and the hesitation you displayed', retorted the master, 'cost you your position as head master of the style'.

And from that time on, the saying 'don't paint legs on a snake' is meant to indicate not to try and improve upon something that is already perfect or understandable.

The Impact of Bruce Lee

The name of Bruce Lee is synonymous with Chinese kung fu; irrespective of his media success, he was responsible for creating a kung fu style in his own right. This style known as *jeet kune-do* or 'way of the intercepting fist', was formulated partly in his early youth through the study of wing chun under grandmaster Yip Man and merging it with certain western boxing styles and also including Thai boxing techniques. This system was so innovative because it broke down certain barriers between eastern and western fighting systems. In simple terms, it was as though he had combed through many fighting disciplines, picking up all that was effective and blending them together. Although Bruce Lee's untimely death was felt the world over, the legacy he left inspired martial artists everywhere and his style of jeet kune-do is enthusiastically practised on every continent in the world today.

The Power of Chi

Just as the karate adept has the capability of breaking objects, so too has kung fu. To break any object with force requires a great deal of strength. When a kung fu practitioner is faced with something to be broken, he summons up a powerful unseen force that lies within him. This intrinsic energy, or vital air, is called *chi*. Chi energy is developed in virtually every kung fu style practised today. Some adepts even make a lifelong pursuit of cultivating this force within the body.

The study of this art is known as chi-gung. Apart from giving its user phenomenal strength, it bequeaths to its practitioners good health, sound blood circulation, and a youthful appearance. It is basically a special breathing exercise, but has many complex mental aspects. A master of chi-gung can, at any given moment, direct this invisible energy to any part of his body. In demonstrations, a master has held his palms uppermost, and within minutes his hands have began to radiate heat – not just warmth but real heat.

In order to develop this chi energy, great concentration is required. It has been said that masters in ancient China could summon their chi so quickly and direct it to any part of the body, that if they were attacked with a bladed weapon, the blade would not be able to penetrate the skin. Even in modern times demonstrations using sharpened meat cleavers have been seen. A member of the audience has attempted to cut through a chi-gung master's skin with a cleaver, but after five minutes or so, making no impression, has given up.

One of the hardest materials to break is stone. Manufactured paving stone and house bricks can all be broken with a fair amount of pressure and know-how. But a rounded stone formed in the earth is another matter altogether. However, in a recent kung fu demonstration, one master not only broke a stone using the side of his hand, but he also sliced the stone into three pieces, much to the amazement of his audience.

Other astounding feats abound in the martial arts world. There was the case of the slim young lady lying on her back and allowing a 200-pound man to jump off a table and land with both feet squarely on her tummy. By directing her chi to that area, she resisted the impact without harm. In another demonstration, a small bed of nails was placed sharp end down on a practitioner's stomach, while he lay prone. Then seven house bricks were stacked on top of the bed of nails. One of the master's students took a huge hammer and began to pound at the bricks, until every one of them was broken. Clearing away the debris, the master calmly rose to his feet, moved the bed of nails away from his stomach, and showed that there was not a mark on him – not even the slightest indentation.

In a chi-gung mind control exercise, another master stacked up five bricks, and announced that he would break all of them except the middle one. Sure enough, when the break was done, all the bricks crumbled into dust – all that is, except the specified middle one. Feats such as these have to be witnessed to be fully appreciated.

In England, a Thai boxing master walked onto the demonstration floor at a national tournament. He placed a large wooden board on the floor, opened a bag containing about half-a-dozen Coca Cola bottles, and began to break them with a hammer. The broken glass spread all over the board, the sharp jagged ends sticking up into the air. Standing up, the master then poured gasoline over the broken bottles and set the whole lot alight. Calmly he walked into this inferno and began to perform techniques. In one such movement he raised his leg into the air way above his head. The supporting leg scrunched sickeningly into the jagged glass, with flames leaping and dancing over the flesh. After about two minutes he stepped off the burning glass with not a mark, cut, or burn on his person. How can it be explained? Some people describe such demonstrations as sensational tricks. But if they defy the laws of science, can they be called tricks?

The Death Touch

It is widely believed among many practitioners of kung fu that if the body is struck at a certain time of day, in some vital area in a certain manner, a chain reaction would start within the body, delaying the effect of the blow for anything up to a few months. After that the victim would die. This is known as *dim mak*, or 'death touch'. It is a very controversial subject even among kung fu masters. The principle is supposed to work on the same lines as acupuncture. The assassin strikes, the victim feels no immediate effects, and thinks he is unharmed. But in a few days or weeks he dies or becomes seriously ill. The majority of the tien hsueh arts (dim mak) are almost extinct. Only a handful of masters still possess the complete methods, and none are willing to part with the knowledge.

Iron Palm

Another lethal practice in kung fu is a specialized technique known as iron palm. Its practitioner can kill with a single blow. The entire forearm must be conditioned gradually over a period of several years. Training for the this technique involves punching bags filled with sand, then later with pebbles and finally with iron filings or metal shot. To aid a student of iron palm in his build-up of hand conditioning, a special ointment is used called dit da jow, made from an ancient recipe. Handed down in Chinese families from generation to generation, it is applied externally, after first being heated. It is said to help prevent bruising and internal injuries, while at the same time strengthening the skin, muscle, and bone. No iron palm practitioner would attempt to train without first using this ointment.

Every master has his own recipe, and only he himself knows the ingredients. Once treated with this, a student begins a set of exercises aimed at building up his chi power.

The ancient masters say that iron palm training is like a man paddling a boat up a river against the current. If he stops paddling even for a second , the boat doesn't stay still, it slips back. Then it takes him a long time to regain the position that he was in before he stopped paddling.

Day by day, the bag training on the iron sand is practised and the iron palm medicine is applied. This goes on for two years and is then stopped. From then on the student trains with punches into thin air, rather like shadow boxing. At this point the chi energy begins to grow on a larger scale. The practitioner returns to the iron-sand bags only about once a month. The picture begins to emerge; the hard sand bags and the soft air, the yin and the yang, the positive and the negative, two opposites uniting to make a whole, the very essence of the tao.

Curing the Sick

Once proficient in iron palm, an adept can kill a person without so much as marking the body, yet cause massive internal damage to the vital organs. In ancient China many a political figure from the emperor's court was mysteriously killed in this way. Nowadays, iron palm is used to cure the sick and injured. This is achieved by the chi kung master generating his chi power and touching and vibrating various vital points on the body, to facilitate a recovery. In many cases the recovery is permanent. This touching is actually the master performing chi transference, using his powerful internal forces to unblock the chi energy channels of the sick people.

It is not uncommon to find that most masters of kung fu are also accomplished doctors of traditional Chinese herbal medicine. Medication, bone-setting, and massage all go hand-in-hand with kung fu. Many teachers have also studied acupuncture, and are well versed in the ailments of the human body.

The Influence of Religion

In China, religion was instrumental in the development of the martial arts. Three great religions flourished. There was Confucianism: an austere doctrine of doing the right and proper thing. Based upon the teachings and analects of the Chinese philosopher Confucius, it is not strictly a religion as we in the West would see it. Confucianism taught duty to parents, devotion to family tradition and a dedication to truth and idealism. This mainly aristocratic philosophy found great appeal among the mandarins and intellectuals but had little to offer the ordinary peasant.

Buddhism

Buddhism arrived in China from India. This religion became divided into various sects, until eventually the original Buddhism as practised in India was barely recognizable. One particular branch of Buddhism that was to have a profound effect upon the martial arts became established at the Shaolin temple called Ch'an: this later gave birth to the Zen Buddhism of Japan. Followers of Ch'an or Zen believe that the centre for meditation and the seat of mental power is the *tan t'ien* or tanden, which is a point situated about two inches (5cm) below the navel. In the internal systems of kung fu, it is believed that this is the place where the vital chi energy gathers.

The Empty Cup

The philosophy of Zen has a deep significance when applied to the martial arts. A beginner enters the place of training with a head full of opinions and thoughts, but part of the discipline is to empty the mind so as to become a vehicle for new learning, in essence to be open-minded.

There is a story about an old Japanese Zen master who was engaged in conversation with a prospective student. The student chatted on and on, full of his own opinions and ideas. He described to the master everything he knew about Zen, trying to impress the old man with his great knowledge. The master sat and listened patiently for a while, then suggested that they take some tea. The student held out his cup dutifully and the master began to pour. The tea came to the top of the cup, but still the master kept on pouring. The tea overflowed but still the master kept on. The student unable to contain himself, pointed out that no more tea would go into the cup. The master looked up and said 'Like this cup you are full of your own desires and ambitions. How then can I show you Zen unless you first empty your cup ?'

The Taoist Legacy

For the Chinese peasants the religion they found affinity with was Taoism. The Taoist idea is yielding, or non-action. Its aim is to achieve a peaceful mind without the extremes of either anger or happiness, a mind without worry. Through these ideas, and the exercises that are their material expression, a good healthy and long life can be achieved. Exercise on a regular basis promotes good health and a healthy body works harder and longer. So the peasant farmers produced a greater yield of crops, thus becoming richer. Although legend suggests that all Chinese martial arts came from Shaolin, it can be seen that in many villages across the country various disciplines which were invaluable to the practice of the arts were already a way of life.

Harmony of Yin And Yang

A fundamental teaching of the Taoist religion is that there is a natural harmony of all things, that everything in existence has its complementary opposite. These two opposing forces that flow into one another in a continuous state of change are known as Yin and Yang, and they are represented by two symbols within a circle. Yin is the negative aspect of the universe and relates to female, night, cold and it is seen as a black fish with a white eye in the circular diagram. Yang is the positive aspect of the universe, indicating the male, day, warmth. It is represented as a white fish with a black eye. Neither can exist without the other. These two inseparable forces are, according to the Taoists, the principle of the universe. The complementary forces flow into one another. Night becomes day, summer becomes winter, hard becomes soft;

the Yin becomes the Yang, continually pushing forwards and the yang becomes yin again. These two apparent opposites were not viewed as permanent and irreconcilable, but constantly changing in a ceaseless rhythmic cycle. Understanding this interchange of Yin and Yang is perhaps the most important single aspect in the learning of a kung fu system.

As the Chinese martial arts are all based on either the nature of soft or hard, action or non-action, it can be realized why the philosophy of Taoism played such an important role in their development. Even today the principles of Taoism permeate the martial arts. The country of South Korea, predominantly Buddhist, has as its national flag the Yin and Yang symbols surrounded by eight trigrams.

Jiu-Jitsu, Judo, Aikido

Jiu-Jitsu, Judo, Aikido

Seek not to know the answers but to understand the questions.

Jiu-Jitsu

Jiu-jitsu in its fullest form was an art of combat used by the samurai warrior. The art dates back to antiquity, being known under the various names of *tai-jutsu*, *yawara* and *hakuda*. Jiu jitsu includes both armed and unarmed techniques. It is regarded as the grandfather of aikido and judo. Within its system lies a variety of skills, from striking vital points and kicking, to strangling and joint locking techniques. It has been said that jiu-jitsu was first practised some 2000 years ago, and many believe it to be the father of all Japanese martial arts.

Traditionally the samurai would only grapple if all else failed. The classical warrior fought in armour, so the empty hand skills looked a little robotic in their execution. When an unseated horseman was fighting without weapons, he would unbalance his adversary and secure him with a lock or grip. This would give him enough time to pull out his short dagger, and thrust it through a chink in the armour to strike a vital point.

In Japan, between the 17th and 19th centuries, the samurai began to fit into a more peaceful environment, devoid of the earlier bloody civil struggles. The samurai often had trouble when attacked by bandits or lawless samurai (*ronin*). The need for empty hand techniques grew and when the samurai were forbidden to wear swords in 1876, it became imperative.

The Samurai Code

Jiu-jitsu was as much a weapon of the samurai as was the sword. The warriors were trained in the techniques of arm-locking and bone-breaking from a very early age. Every samurai was trained in the throws and grappling movements of jiu-jitsu. The samurai had special charts drawn up showing the vital areas of the human body, with the special one-punch killer blows marked out. These charts had been compiled over a period of time, and were tested on condemned prisoners.

The fear of death had no place in the samurai's heart, for he followed a strict code of discipline called *bushido*, 'the warrior way'. This was a moral code of loyalty, duty, and obedience, which had been developed to set a high standard in the training of warriors in the martial arts. It could be likened to the chivalrous code of the knights in feudal Europe. But in effect it was much more than this. The code was a guideline for the samurai's daily behaviour. Should a warrior step outside these rules, he would be expected to discipline himself accordingly, even to the supreme and ultimate act of committing *seppuku* (the formal name for *hara-kiri*). To a samurai, fighting was his only vocation, and in some cases it could even be described as an obsession.

When the samurai of feudal Japan weren't involved in one of the many wars of that period, they spent their leisure time immersed in martial activities, for their sporting ends. But even then, the strict code still applied. They placed great emphasis on victory in combat, whether for real or not. It was not unusual for exponent to go to a sporting session and never return. Many deaths resulted from dangerous techniques used in these so-called leisure sports.

The teachings of Zen Buddhism were of great importance to the samurai too. It was a faith which taught that salvation came not from some faraway god but from within the individual himself. The idea that a man could influence his own destiny appealed to men who lived with warfare and death on a daily basis.

Legend of the Willow Tree

There is one legend that was verbally handed down, that relates the story of a Japanese Physician who lived in Nagasaki named Akiyama. He had travelled to China to learn new techniques in medicine. While there he learned an art known as hakuda, which consisted of kicking and striking plus seizing and grappling. Akiyama also learned 28 different ways of recovering a man from apparent death. Upon his return to Japan, the doctor began to teach this art to a few selected students, but because he had only a few techniques, his students soon got bored and left him. Very much annoyed about this, Akiyama went to the Tenjin shrine for a hundred days to meditate and worship. During this period, he is said to have discovered 303 different methods of the art. This multiplication of techniques was brought about because Akiyama had seen a pine tree standing erect in the forest which was broken to pieces during a violent snow storm. Yet a willow tree nearby yielded to the weight of the snow on its branches and did not break. He took this lesson and applied it to the art he had brought from China. He opened another school which was very successful, naming it *yoshin-ryu* or 'willow tree school'.

History records that many skills of grappling and throwing abounded in Japan, as long ago as a thousand years. These methods were systematized as jiu-jitsu in 1532 by Hisamori Takenouchi. They formed an integral part of the samurais' training and served as a complement to their more specialized weapon skills. Within this art of jiu-jitsu lay armed as well as unarmed techniques. Use was made of such weapons as the *naginata*, 'bo staff' and *yari*, 'spear'. All stressed, as might be expected from skills developed by warriors, maximum effectiveness on the battlefield. Jiu-jitsu is often identified as pure grappling with the involvement of arm-locks and joint manipulations, but what is perhaps not so well known is that the art also includes kicks and punches. It is thought that these were introduced from the martial arts systems of southern China. Another aspect of jiu-jitsu was that of *atemi*, the art of attacking pressure points, joints and other vulnerable areas.

Jiu-jitsu is not a contest of muscular strength – in fact this is not a major factor at all. The art relies on balance, leverage and speed to effect the necessary movements, and then available strength is applied to its greatest advantage. Jiu-jitsu tends to wipe out the differences of size, weight, height and reach, thus evening the odds and making the art popular and accessible to women.

The Secret Art of Resuscitation

Kuatsu is the ancient art of resuscitation or revival, itself a branch of jiu-jitsu. It is so highly specialized that years of thorough training were given to instructors who had been carefully selected. They learned the art under a strict oath of secrecy. Kuatsu was considered to be the supreme knowledge in jiu-jitsu. It was customary for those who received the secret knowledge to pay the master a sum of money.

Methods of kuatsu are numerous and vary from school to school. One of the simplest methods used for resuscitating those who have been temporarily suffocated by choking involves grabbing the patient from the back and placing the edge of the palms on the abdomen, pushing upwards in a sharp movement. Groin injuries can be put to rights using methods of kuatsu, although severe blows and strangulations require more complicated methods of recovery. It is thought that the knowledge of kuatsu stems from the sister art of acupuncture, that of *shiatsu*.

The Modern Outlook

The emphasis in jiu-jitsu today is on dislocation of a joint or limb by means of locks or leverage grips. In other words, exponents of the art don't go all the way. The locks are so complete in themselves that the mere threat of damage which their application implies, is sufficient to induce even the most hardened opponent to cry for mercy.

Jitsu means 'art' or 'skill' and *jiu* means 'gentle' or 'soft'. Thus, freely translated, jiu-jitsu is the gentle art, although one would not think so to see skilled practitioners in Japan weighing a little more than 120 pounds throwing burly westerners about like rag dolls.

Although jiu-jitsu is strictly a martial art, it has been developed as a competitive sport. When fighting at world class level, because of its competitive aspects jiu-jitsu has had to have many of its lethal techniques deleted because otherwise the world's arenas would be littered with dead bodies.

Many staunch traditionalists refuse to take part in active competition because they feel that the competitive fighting concept is diluting the classical martial way of jiu-jitsu.

Judo

Judo is the modern sports form of jiu jitsu. It was developed by Professor Jigoro Kano in 1882 in Suidobashi, Tokyo. It is a well organized system of unarmed techniques, primarily based on leverage, throws and holds. Judo is not a jitsu art. It has been developed as a sport rather than any kind of martial art involving lethal or serious injury. The word *judo* means 'gentle way'.

The Sickly Youth

Outside of China, judo is perhaps the most widely practised of all the martial arts. It is viewed variously as a sport, a fighting art, a spiritual discipline and an excellent form of physical education. The latter was the primary intention of its founder, who believed that healthy individuals would promote mutual welfare for the ultimate benefit of the nation.

As a youth Kano suffered from ill health and at school he was constantly bullied, so in a concerted effort to combat this he embarked on his own programme of fitness training. Being born after the end of Japan's feudal era, Kano had ample opportunity to sample many of the western world's sports that were being newly introduced to his country. By the time Kano was 17 he decided to study martial arts. Jiu-jitsu looked the obvious choice so he enrolled under the tutelage of Hachinosuke Fukoda of the Tenjin Shinyo school. This school specialized in *atemiwaza* or 'striking techniques' and also *newaza* or 'grappling methods'. The severity of the training took its toll upon Kano, who over a period of time received many injuries. He treated these himself with an odious liquid bought from the village herbalist.

Upon his teacher's death Kano looked around for another school and he joined the kito-ryu which specialized in *nagewaza* or 'throwing techniques'. His thirsty mind drank in everything the school had to offer. Then in 1882 Kano founded his own style, to be known as Kano-ryu, but it was later changed to Kodokan judo. Establishing himself at a temple in a poor quarter of Tokyo he began to teach his style to just nine students. During this time he was awarded his master's rank in kito-ryu jiu-jitsu. A challenge from another school was met, and Kano fought and beat the great champion Fukushima. Because of this the Tenshin Shinyo school also awarded him a master's degree. Kano's name was now beginning to attract attention.

In 1886 the Japanese police force held a grand tournament in which all the jiu-jitsu schools were invited to participate in order to see which of the schools would prevail. With a team of 15 hand picked judoka the Kodokan judo school won 13 of the 15 matches, establishing their supremacy once and for all. Kano's new art was recognized by the Japanese government and also the Butokukwai, the governing body for martial arts.

Fundamentals of the Sport

A person trained in judo has the skill and ability to beat another equally or more highly skilled player in competition. One who practises the skill of judo, is called a *judoka*. The method of winning in competition is defined in a mutually accepted system of rules laid down by the organizing body. Judo techniques are divided into the three categories: *tachiwaza,* 'standing techniques'; *new-aza,* 'ground techniques'; and *atemiwaza,* 'vital point techniques'. Within these three categories are many subdivisions that encompass the whole periphery of judo techniques.

Similar to karate, the judo grading is based upon both proficiency in contest and on knowledge of the art. Differentiations in rank are shown by the coloured belts worn by the judoka. Beginners start with a white belt and graduate to yellow, orange, green, blue and then brown belt. Ultimately, the student advances to shodan or first degree black belt. The dan grades range from first to tenth dan. Although it is possible to attain a twelfth dan, no one has actually ever achieved this rank, save for the founder, Jigoro Kano.

About 70 to 80 percent of judo training consists of *randori* or 'free sparring', in which two contestants practise throwing and grappling under the conditions of actual contest. Randori is usually two judoka attacking and defending at will.

To practise judo the student wears a uniform of white with a kimono-style top and trousers, referred to as a *judogi.* A bow is exchanged between jodoka at the beginning and end of each practice session.

Aikido

Aikido was founded by Morihei Ueshiba in 1942. *Aikido* means 'the way of harmony'. In this art there is no actual attack as such, the basic ethic being defence first. As a teenager Ueshiba had almost died as a result of a bout of scarlet fever. In an effort to build back his strength, he enrolled in yagyu shinkage ryu jiu-jitsu. At the outbreak of the Russo-Japanese war, Ueshiba was conscripted into the army. This experience gave him ample opportunity to travel and study other forms of martial arts and combat methods.

Returning home after the war, Ueshiba was made a master instructor with the title Menkyo-kaiden, which is the highest licence of proficiency. After that achievement he began to travel all around Japan trying out other systems. In 1915 he began studies in yet another style of jiu-jitsu, that of *daito-ryu,* under the great master Sokaku. But Ueshiba became dissatisfied with the strictly militaristic styles he had been learning and being a man of an intense poetic nature left to seek his own higher ideals.

The death of his father in 1920 came as a great shock and left Ueshiba in a state of psychological distress. He sought the spiritual guidance of a priest named Deguchi of the Omoto sect (a branch of Shintoism). Under the priest's guidance he meditated and studied philosophy. It was during this period living in close harmony to nature that he is said to have had a vision of enlightenment.

Ueshiba's Vision

Apparently Ueshiba had just finished a period of intense meditation. Walking out into a small yard he knelt to take a drink. Suddenly the ground began to tremble, causing ripples in the soil. Right in front of him a stream of vapour shot out of the ground like a geyser. He was bathed in a golden liquid which covered his whole body. His body felt light as though he were floating and the laws of gravity seemed not to exist. Voices were ringing in his ears, but as he looked around he could only see the birds chirping. At that moment Morihei Ueshiba knew that he and the universe were entwined. The message he received was that the fundamental principle of the martial arts was love and not combat, love of the universal kind. The martial arts of the true way were not about brute force and injury, but harmony and the promotion of the *ki* (an intrinsic energy similar to the chi). This revelation changed Ueshiba's thinking dramatically and was to be the foundation that aikido was built upon.

Returning to Tokyo, Ueshiba opened his first dojo in 1927. In February 1942 aikido was officially recognized as the name of his new art. Thus, with his 'way of harmony', Ueshiba accomplished his burning desire to keep alive the legacy of budo in the modern world.

The Aims of Aikido

Training in aikido differs from training in other Japanese martial arts. It is necessary to understand not only the unique movements and techniques of the art, but also the deep underlying philosophy that teaches adepts to master the mind, develop the character, and cultivate to a high degree the art of living in harmony with everyday circumstances. Aikido's primary objective is to unify mind, body, and the mysterious force know as ki. The ki is the very soul of aikido, and it can be loosely described as a super force or power that is inherent in every human being – a souped-up source of pure energy, waiting to be developed and then tapped.

Aikido in Action

Aikido techniques use an element of compliance such as is found in jiu-jitsu. The attacker lunges forwards, so the defender, using his aikido skills, will harmonize with the movement and seek to redirect it. For instance, if someone were to pull at you, you can either resist, in which case the stronger of the two will prevail, or you can suddenly go in the direction you are being pulled. The effect of this is to unbalance the attacker, making him open to your next planned response.

The *aikidoka,* one skilled in aikido, performs his movements with a very fluid motion. To compete or fight in aikido takes much more skill than is found in any of the other striking martial arts.

Unlike judo and jiu-jitsu, an aikido practitioner does not wear the traditional suit as seen in the other two arts. Instead, he wears a garb known as *hakama,* which is a long split skirt covering the legs down to the feet. One of the reasons for wearing the hakama is so that no one will be able to observe the foot movements.

The Mystic and Ki

When the founder of aikido was in his mid-eighties, he began to get the reputation of being something of a mystic, because of the many unexplained feats he performed to demonstrate the power of the ki force within him.

On one occasion when Ueshiba, who stood only five feet tall and weighed a mere 120 pounds, gave a demonstration of his art in front of two dozen or so newspapermen, he called for six volunteers to attack him. Six men of various sizes and weights stepped up to accept the challenge. The great teacher told all the men to attack him simultaneously. When they did so, the old man, hardly moving, sent his would-be assailants flying in all directions.

Before the demonstration, Ueshiba had drawn a small chalk circle around his feet to prove to the onlookers that little movement was required to effect the technique. As the six men got up from the ground everyone looked to

Ueshiba, whose feet still remained firmly planted within that circle.

At another time, Ueshiba wanted to demonstrate the positive attitude that the ki force creates. He told an audience that he could will himself to become two-thirds lighter than his own body weight. He next took 20 teacups, filled them with tea, and arranged them with their saucers in a circle. Stepping up onto the rim of the first tea cup, he commenced to walk round the complete circle of cups, on the rims. When he had finished, no tea had been spilled in the saucers, and none of the delicate china cups had been cracked or broken. This, he explained, was ki in action.

Another very famous story relating to Ueshiba, describes how, in front of television cameras, he invited four men to see if they could lift him from the ground. Bearing in mind that Ueshiba was in his eighties and weighed little more than 120 pounds, this would seem an easy task. The old man stood silently and concentrated his ki energy downwards towards the ground. The four men walked up, put their arms around his waist and lifted. Try as they would, they could not budge this frail old man from the spot. Eventually, the four men decided that two would grab his feet, and two would lift him from the waist in one co-ordinated movement. And still they failed, much to their amazement. The old man remained rooted to the spot.

The Major Schools of Aikido

Although Morihei Ueshiba was the founder of modern aikido, there are more than 30 distinct styles of the art. Most founders of the other systems were pupils of the great Ueshiba. Kenji Tomiki was the first of Ueshiba's students to be awarded his eighth dan black belt. Tomiki aikido, named after him, is a style that stresses competition. He believed, unlike Ueshiba, that his students would gain mental improvement if they engaged in techniques during active freestyle competition. Another style is yoshinkan aikido, devised by Gozo Shioda, another former pupil of Ueshiba. Yoshinkan style was the form the Tokyo police adopted for the training of their officers. Today Shioda has more than 200 black belt instructors teaching city police forces throughout Japan.

Aikido Conclusion

Although, on the face of it, aikido is a splendid system for self-defence, it is its deep philosophy of life that sets it apart from the other Japanese martial arts. The central aim of aikido is self-realization through discipline. This discipline begins with the learning of the correct use of physical energy in the aikido movements. Harmony of body and mind gradually develops with practice, and as the desire for immediate results falls away, the process of realization begins. It was the founder himself who said 'Aikido has no end – there's just the beginning and further growth'.

Other Forms of Japanese Martial Arts

Other Forms of Japanese Martial Arts

It is no disgrace to lose,
if one has sought to win.

The field of Japanese martial arts covers many interesting subjects. In the popularity stakes, judo and karate are the front runners, but there is a multitude of lesser known arts that are practised with the same fervour and dedication. In times gone by, some of these martial arts were actual battlefield skills. Today in an age of push-button technology, they have been relegated to the status of hobbies or pastimes. But a few are alive and very much as deadly as they were 500 years ago. They are practised by a few devoted traditionalists whose aim is to keep alive the skills of their ancestors.

Sumo: The Indigenous Art of Japan

Nowhere else in the world can be found an art quite like sumo. It is strictly an indigenous art or sport belonging to

Japan and consists of two huge man mountains trying to push each other out of a wrestling ring.

Sumo wrestlers compete on a dirt mound called a *dohyo*, which is 15 feet in diameter. A contestant loses immediately if any part of his body, other than the soles of his feet, scrapes or lands on the surface of the dohyo.

The Blink of an Eye

The whole subject of sumo wrestling is steeped in Shintoism, Shinto being one of the religions of Japan. Because of the nature of the contest, a match only lasts a few seconds – it's all over in the blink of an eye.

There is much ceremony and formality, which to Western eyes seems endless. There are 48 classical throws that can end a sumo match, and contests that last longer than a minute are extremely rare. A sumo wrestler has no right of protest, the decision of the referee being final. There are no tied matches, and in the case of a close contest when it has been difficult to determine the winner, a re-match is ordered. Sumo is the only body contact sport in which there are no weight groups.

Sumo History

Japanese legend tells of the first ever sumo match, which was supposedly held when the god Takemikazuchi won a bout with the leader of a rival tribe. The first matches were a form of ritual dedicated to the gods. In those days it was known as *sumai*, and fights were often fought to the death. Fighters wear a silk loin cloth called a *mawashi*, which is 10 yards long and 2 feet wide. It is folded, then wrapped around the waist of the wrestler. A fighter begins each contest by stamping his feet. This is to drive away all the evil spirits from the ring (sumo wrestlers are very superstitious). They also extend their hands to indicate that they bear no concealed weapons.

In 1852, when Commodore Matthew Perry arrived in Japan from the United States in his 'black ships', attempting to open up Japan, which had been in self-imposed isolation for over two hundred years, to Western trade and diplomatic relations, the authorities made certain that on the shore to greet him were the top sumo men of the day. This gesture was to show the unwelcome Americans that they should by no means underestimate the stature of the Japanese nation.

Modern Sumo Matches

Today in Japan, sumo is both a professional and an amateur sport. A series of 15 day tournaments are held six times a year. All matches begin from a crouch position. Before a bout takes place there is a lengthy pre-fight ritual. At one point the wrestler grabs a handful of salt and tosses it into the ring as an act of purification. Unless he is familiar with the traditions of the Shinto religion, many of these pre-fight rituals are completely meaningless to the visiting Westerner. Hundreds of years ago women participated in the matches, but these days all that has been banned.

Feats of Strength

The prime requisite in sumo wrestling is strength. The hips are the centre of balance and leverage for the sumo man. When this balance is combined with bodyweight, flexibility, speed and strength, the sumo wrestler is virtually immovable. Strange as it may seem, a sumo wrestler can do a complete side split until he sits, flat on the ground, even though he carries a weight of more than 350 pounds. Stories are told of a sumo wrestler who stood in front of an army jeep, braced himself, and told the driver to accelerate. Although the tires churned away furiously and the smell of burning rubber filled the air, the giant wrestler stood his ground as solid as a rock, and the jeep could not move. Sometimes, the wrestlers will invite five or six men from the audience to have a go at trying to push them over, and the volunteers seldom succeed.

Unwritten Laws of Sumo Wrestling

Although the rules in a Sumo match are relatively few, there is a certain sumo code that is strictly adhered to. In the *yokozuna*, 'grand champion' class, the wrestler must be able continually to demonstrate his superiority. If a grand champion loses more that eight bouts in a tournament he will voluntarily retire. This is the unspoken rule of all yokozunas.

The sumo wrestler's topknot is not applied until the wrestler reaches the makuuchi division. Then his hair will not be cut until he retires from sumo.

The sumo wrestler's ritual of scattering salt in the ring before the fight must take at least four minutes. He is judged by the audience as to how he performs this rite. It is up to each novice sumo wrestler to take responsibility for his own eating habits.

Kyudo: the Way of the Bow

Archery played a major part in ancient Japanese warfare, and the art of *kyujutsu* was developed as a means of perfecting combat techniques with bow and arrow. When peace finally settled on Japan the *jutsu* arts became *do* arts. Jutsu referred to feudal combative skills, where the aim was to kill. A do form is a road, path, or way. It is a means to a way or method of promoting self-understanding and perfection through martial skills.

Thus the kyujutsu of the battlefield became the kyudo of today, although the ancient rituals and ceremony involved in the art have never altered.

Kyudo Doctrine

Linked very closely to the study of Zen, kyudo is a highly formalized martial art in which the ultimate aim for the archer is to compete and overcome himself. With proper concentration, man and bow fuse together until they are one. Then and only then, at the right instant, will the arrow be automatically released. Kyudo is not all about hitting the bullseye, or for that matter the target. The important point is how the shooting is done, and the archer's state of mind when the arrow is released. Kyudo of Japan is a combination of the physical art with the philosophical principles of Zen Buddhism. There is perhaps more emphasis placed on the Zen concept, in Japanese archery, than in all the other martial arts save maybe for kendo.

The Bow and Arrow

Unlike its European counterpart, the kyudo bow is an unusual size and shape. It is more than six feet long and is constructed entirely of bamboo, fashioned to the same traditional design of the samurai who originally used it so well. It has a weight pull of around 80 pounds. The bow grip is not centred, like the old English longbow, but is placed approximately one-third of the distance from the bottom of the bow. The kyudo bow is the longest in the world. The length of the arrows range from three feet to three-and-a-half feet. The bowstring is made from hemp. A quiver is never used in kyudo, the archer preferring to hold a second arrow in his bowstring hand.

Robin Hood of Japan

Just as England had its Robin Hood and Switzerland its William Tell, Japan had its great archer hero, named Nasu no Yoichi. In 1280, when the warlike clans of Japan were struggling for supremacy, two great clans met in what was to be a decisive battle. It occurred along the coast of Japan's Inland Sea, at a place called Yashima. One of the clans, the Genji, had managed to drive the enemy forces, the Heike clan, into the sea. From the bridge of his ship the Heike lord hoisted a beautiful golden fan with the royal crest upon it. The fan flickered from the mast in the wind. He laughingly challenged the Genji samurai on the beach to shoot it down. Nasu no Yoichi accepted the challenge.

Taking careful aim, he focused on the barely visible target that was bobbing and fluttering with the movement of the ship. After what seemed like minutes, Nasu released his arrow. It sailed 400 yards (so legend says), and suddenly found its mark in the centre pin where the fine ribs of the fan were held together. The golden fan split into pieces and dropped into the sea. The Heike soldiers were completely dismayed at this bad omen. The samurai of the Genji clan, after witnessing such an incredible feat of marksmanship, began their attack with renewed zeal and the Heike clan were crushed completely.

Kyudo Today

Kyudo is practised by more than half a million Japanese today. It is a great favourite with women because it is thought to enhance grace and manners.

Those who embrace the art of kyudo as their way of enlightenment must be prepared for years of training. Traditionally, a student will be taught to breathe properly, how to relax, how to adopt the correct posture, how to let his mind take over. All this is learned for nearly 18 months, before he is ever allowed to shoot his first arrow. Although much has been said of the Zen concept in kyudo, in a lighter vein it is also a practical sport. Competitors do their best to score a bull. This side to kyudo resembles Western archery, but is frowned upon by the ardent traditionalists.

The Naginata: Women's Weapon of Self-Defence

Naginata, to all intents and purposes, is a female sport. The naginata is a type of halberd that foot soldiers used on the battlefields of Japan more than 500 years ago.

…cent times, it has become a popular sport among …women of Japan. It is even taught in girl's high …ools up and down the country. Today the live blade …as been replaced by an angled piece of plaited bamboo. In wielding the naginata, the motions are circular and flowing, not sharp and straight. This makes for flexibility and suppleness, and helps tone up the body. Naginata takes much less strength to practise than kendo, hence its overwhelming popularity with women.

The Battlefield Weapon

The art of the naginata dates back to when foot soldiers used to mount short swords on poles. This enabled them to take a swipe at the legs of horses in an effort to unseat their riders. Eventually the naginata became a standard weapon in warfare. When the wars ceased, a shortened version of the weapon was kept in every samurai's home. This was intended for use by the woman of the house should she be attacked or burglarized while the master was out in the service of his lord. Japanese homes being small and low-ceilinged, it was not easy for the occupant to wield a large weapon. So the shortened naginata was introduced for use by women.

Naginata Equipment

In the practice of naginata-do, to give it the correct term, the old standard six-and-a-half-foot weapon is used. Each end is covered with a leather tip. A face mask, the same as that used in kendo, called a *men*, is employed by the ladies for protection. This, combined with a special breastplate, arm and shin guards, and a girdle of protective padding, completes the uniform.

The sport form of naginata-do has mushroomed since introduction of tournament competition in the 1960s.

Iai-do: the Skill of the Quick Draw Sword

Iai-do is the art of the quick draw, using a *katana* or samurai sword. It was developed into a do form from the old skill of iai-jutsu, in which the samurai would draw his sword upon a sudden encounter, and slay the enemy who had tried to ambush him. It can be likened to the technique of the old fast-draw gunfighters in westerns. A man named Hayashizaki Jinsuke formulated this quick-draw style in the mid-16th century. As a result, he founded the famous schools of muso shinden ryu.

Modern Martial Discipline

Today, iai-do is a form of martial training that is practised alone. Once a student has received the correct tuition, the rate of improvement depends entirely upon himself. Much ceremony is accorded to the placing of the sheathed sword into the belt or *obi*. There is a certain aspect of Zen in this procedure. Constant practice and understanding of the traditions behind the art is needed before an adept is ready to try out the fast draw. In the past, western students who tried to rush the training and mental discipline often regretted it, because in doing so they severed their fingers and in some cases the whole of the hand on the razor-sharp edge of the sword blade. Iai-do is a noncombative art.

Shorinji Kempo

Shorinji kempo is a martial art that developed 1000 years ago at the Shaolin temple. One may think for that reason that it is a kung fu system, but it is not. Shorinji kempo is the Japanese reading of Shaolin fist. The whole system was rinsed through, with techniques being added, others being dropped and restyled, to become known as shorinji kempo. It was devised by Michiomi Nakano, who later became known as Doshin So. It began life, in the modern context, just after World War Two, in Japan. The system has at the core, a form of Buddhism known as Kongo Zen. The philosophy embraced within this system encourages self-help, and teaches that man's individual progress through life is dependent on his own efforts. Although the art claims Chinese ancestry, many of its movements resemble jiu-jitsu and aiki-jitsu. The principles of shorinji place equal emphasis on the use of both soft and hard techniques.

The Black Dragon Society

The founder of shorinji, Doshin So, spent much of his life in Manchuria under the patronage of Mitsuru Toyama, the founder of the secret society known as the Black Dragon. This was an organization set on promoting political unrest in Asia. In his twenties Doshin So was sent to China to spy for the Japanese government. While he was there he visited the old Shaolin temple, and at once was greatly impressed with the martial techniques of the monks. He began to practise martial arts eagerly, and after further travels around China he met many masters of almost extinct systems of kempo and kung fu, and trained with them.

After the war, Doshin So returned to Japan and brought his form of martial art out into the open. He had completely revised, and expanded the original system.

Today there are more than 800 training halls around Japan for shorinji kempo, with 300,000 member students. The aim in kempo is like in other martial arts ultimately spiritual: the pursuit of dharma spirit. The dharma spirit brings the practitioner in touch with the ultimate reality: the middle path of harmony between matter and spirit, body and mind.

Kendo

Kendo, iai-do and naginata-do are severe traditional martial arts that offer their students something that goes far deeper than mere competitive sport. This aspect of the traditional values is probably the underlying motivation that brings most novices into kendo. It is for this reason that kendo instructors remind new students that they must never forget that they are joining a society that tries to follow a very ancient training whose rigours they accept for the moral values that lie behind them.

The Way of the Sword

Traditionally the sword represented the samurai warrior's soul. For someone other than the owner to touch it without permission, even inadvertently, represented a great insult and was often punished by death if the offender was a peasant. If another samurai offended, it could lead to a duel. *Kendo* means 'way of the sword'. Unlike western swordplay, Japanese sword fighting consisted of a series of complicated cuts, or sometimes just one downward slash, to gain victory over an opponent.

Modern Kendo

Early Japanese fencing schools sought to teach effective techniques to train their warriors, without actually using a real blade because mistakes with a real sword during training proved to be quite costly in terms of human life. So the heavy oak *bokken* was invented. This consisted of a piece of hard red oak with the shape, weight, and balance of a real sword. But this, too, caused injuries, some of them fatal. In an attempt to further reduce the injury level, a bamboo sword called a *shinai* was devised. This was made of four pieces of bamboo shaped and fitted together by fiber and encased in animal skin. This shinai is the weapon used in today's modern competition fighting.

Kendo Armour

Kendoka, those who practise kendo, when training or fighting in competition, wear protective armour called *bogu.* This consists of a heavy steel helmet called a *men,* which weighs around six or seven pounds. A breastplate call the *do* and gauntlet-type gloves named *kote* are the basic protection used, together with *tare,* a lower waist protector.

All kendo armour is tremendously expensive, even a cheap outfit being likely to cost many hundreds of pounds. The traditional split skirt, called a *hakama,* completes the kendo fighter's attire.

Basic Movements

Training for kendo requires much physical stamina because the fighter must be able to bear the smashing blows of the shinai. He has to move around with agility, weighed down by all the body armor, and still wield his own weapon at an opponent. Kendo, like any other Oriental fighting discipline, has basic moves which, when used in sequence, become intricate manoevres. One particular movement, called *chiburi*, is where an exponent has imagined he has killed somebody with a sword cut. He has to execute a downward flick with the blade to shake off the victims's blood before returning the sword to the scabbard.

The Master Swordsman

The most renowned swordsman in all Japan was the samurai named Miyamoto Musashi, sometimes called *Kensei*, or sword saint. Born in 1584, Musashi was completely devoted to kendo, and by the age of 30 had fought and won more than 60 contests, killing all his opponents. Musashi pursued the ideal of the warrior searching for enlightenment along the perilous paths of kendo and duelling. Life for him was a series of challenges and obstacles to be overcome.

He was convinced he was invincible, and to all intents and purposes he probably was. He retired to the mountains, during his last years, to formulate a principle of philosophy and strategy. This he wrote down and called *Go Rin No Sho* or 'a book of five rings'. This masterpiece, as it has been called, is today used by Japanese businessmen as a guide to the strategy of pulling off multi-million dollar deals. Musashi died in 1645. Near to his death, he wrote: 'When you have attained the way of strategy there will not be one thing that you cannot understand'.

The Essence of Kendo

It is difficult for the average person to understand the essence of kendo. Its main purpose is not the acquisition of technique but instead directed towards the improvement of spirit and one's moral conduct. All true swordsmen carried with them the concept that technical skill and the development of the spiritual man were inseparable. Even today many kendoka believe that to practise kendo purely as a sport is to pervert its essential purpose.

The Ninja Clans of Death

Ninjutsu means 'stealth art' or 'stealing in'. Its practitioners are called *ninja*. It is said to originate from a Chinese military tactic and guerilla warfare book called *The Art of War*, written in the fourth century by a Chinese general name Sun Tsu. It is assumed that Japanese scholars had read the book during their culture-gathering journeys to China. From these seeds grew the deadly clans that were to be feared throughout Japan for centuries. The most famous ninja clans were born and trained in the Iga and Koga areas of Japan's main island, Honshu. Unlike most espionage systems where recruits were drawn from the military or law enforcement services, the ninja were born into it, coming from what were known as ninja families.

The Foundation of Secrecy

Secrecy was the foundation of the ninja tradition and it was because of this that their training camps and strongholds were always located in remote mountainous regions. It was then that the young ninjas trained from the age of about five. There was no distinction between boys and girls – all had to learn the trade of death. The girls, as they grew older and their female attributes became more obvious, trained in a different way. They were taught the powers of seduction, but still retained the ultimate aim of silent killing. This dreaded secret society of espionage experts cum assassins, would strike fear into the boldest of samurai hearts when known to be working in their particular area. The ninja would creep forth, spilling out of the shadows of the night dressed all in black, and strike his allotted target, which would be either a rich lord or a powerful and important samurai. Then, with the deed done, he would blend back into the night like a phantom.

Feared Throughout the Land

The ninja and their exploits of instant assassination became so talked about, that the peasants, most of whom were uneducated, began to believe that the ninja were ghosts sent from another world just to kill. Stories of ninja assassinations spread like wildfire from village to village and from town to town. And so, for 700 years or more, the mere mention of ninja would turn lord and peasant alike white with terror. Of course, for the ninja this was an ideal situation because fear is a very powerful weapon and worked well for them on many occasions. Stories abounded of how the ninja could walk on water, pass through solid walls, disappear at will, and even change themselves into some horrific demon. The tales were a blend of imagination running riot and greatly exaggerated facts. But for the ninja they worked.

Ninja Training Camps

A young ninja's training began with the basic martial arts. He was required to become proficient to master level with at least four weapons. Early training began with the five basic skills – balance, agility, strength, stamina, and special skills. It was these special skills that put the ninja in a class of his own. This unique and very specialized training had, for the most part, to begin at a very early age when the children's bones and ligaments were soft and pliable. After years of stretching and joint manipulation, a field ninja was capable of dislocating his joints at will. This was particularly useful if he was ever captured and bound. By dislocating certain joints, he could release himself and escape.

Breathing and meditation were also taught. Breath control was paramount for the ninja especially when escaping by water, where it was reputed that a ninja could hold his breath under the surface for as long as three minutes. Also, by means of shallow breathing, he could enter a room full of sleeping men and control his heartbeats so as not to give himself away. A ninja learnt all about woodcraft, tracking, and survival, and was also a competent herbalist, being conversant with the use of poisons and their antidotes.

The Master of Disguise

The ninja served all masters, anyone at all, without discrimination. Their services and skills were for hire to perform any dirty or dangerous task without question. It was not unknown for one ninja clan to be pitted against another. All ninja were accomplished actors and masters of disguise, for the ninja had many roles to play in the practice of his black art. His athletic abilities included being able to run 125 miles in one day and hang from a tree branch for hours at a time. He could climb great heights, swim long distances, and was extremely proficient in unarmed combat.

The Mission

Usually a ninja on a mission carried only what he could safely house upon his person. Shoulder packs or bags would only hamper his movement. But his special garb, that all-black uniform, had many concealed pockets in which he could hide the tools of his trade. These included such items as *shuriken*, the sharp pointed throwing star, often tipped with a deadly poison; dried food for his journey; rope; medicines; and a special claw device made from leather and iron that fitted around his wrists to enable him to climb and grip on hard surfaces such as castle walls. Castles in Japan were made of wood.

The ninja sword, which he usually wore slung over his back, was unlike the samurai's traditional *katana*. It was much shorter in length and had a straighter blade. This gave him greater mobility when fighting in the low-ceilinged Japanese rooms of the feudal era. The scabbard was longer than it needed to be. This enable the ninja to carry items in the detachable bottom of the scabbard.

The Assassination

A ninja sent out to kill someone might have to wait hours,

or even days, before his target came within reach. So all his special skills were needed to prevent his being discovered. In one old legend a ninja was sent out to kill a particular lord. The lord's castle was guarded day and night and virtually impossible to enter. But the ninja still gained entry. After he had sought out his victim, who not unnaturally had a retinue of bodyguards around him, the ninja worked out a plan for the lord's demise. The black-garbed assassin concealed himself under the lord's private toilet and waited for him to come to the only place where he could be sure the lord would be by himself. As the lord entered and performed his daily habit, the ninja pierced his body with a short spear and killed him outright. However fanciful that old story may be, it does at least exemplify the lengths to which a ninja would go to fulfil his task of assassination and murder.

The Ninja Hierarchy

The ninja hierarchy was built up in three tiers. The first were the *jonin*, usually the chiefs or bosses who were at the top of the tree. A step lower down with the *chunin*, the middle-ranking ninja, the go-betweens, the ones whom people approached and paid to get the dirty jobs done. The lowest rung of the ladder was made up of the *genin* or field ninja. They were the ones who carried out most of the work and took all the risks. All ninja took a blood oath of secrecy. If any of them broke this oath they were hunted down and killed mercilessly. If a field agent were ever captured by the enemy he could expect to be horribly tortured and put to death slowly. Because of this, a captured ninja was expected to commit suicide before he could be forced through torture to divulge who had hired him for his mission, or even worse, betray some of the clan's innermost secrets. Yet, knowing that all this could happen to him, the ninja still plied his deadly trade with supreme efficiency.

The Martial Arts of Korea

The Martial Arts of Korea

A steed is not praised for its might,
but for its thoroughbred quality.

Taekwon-do

Taekwon-do is a martial art which was developed independently centuries ago in Korea. In those days it was know as *tae kyon. Tae* means 'to kick or smash with the feet', and *kwon* means 'to punch or destroy with the hand or fist'. *Do* means 'method'.

Taekwon-do is the technique of unarmed combat for self-defence. It has more that 1300 years of history and tradition behind it. A Buddhist monk named Won Kwang is said to have originated the five principles that today form the basis of taekwon-do. The art developed as a means of self-protection for the scattered tribal groups who were under constant threat from the warlike neighbours

This martial art is very much a modern concept, but its roots stretch back over a thousand years or more to the indigenous native style of tae kyon. The name taekwon-do came into being at a conference of masters in 1955, when General Choi Hong Hi submitted this particular name because it closely resembled the old name of tae kyon. The considerable Japanese martial arts influence on taekwon-do is a consequence of their occupation of Korea from 1907 to 1945.

The Three Kingdoms

In the southern part of the Korean Peninsula nearly two thousand years ago, there was a small kingdom called Silla. In those days the Korean peninsula consisted of three kingdoms. The smallest of these was the Silla Kingdom, which was always under attack from its two powerful enemies to the north, Pak-Je and to the west, Koguryu. Because of its geographical location it was also threatened from China and Japan. Matters came to a head in the seventh century when China challenged its most northern neighbour, Koguryu, sending in 300,000 troops. However, the Koguryuans lured the invading Chinese into an ambush on a scale never before seen. The warlike tribes of the Koguryu kingdom put to the sword over 250,000 Chinese troops in a single day.

A few years later, before China could wreak her revenge upon Koguryu, the ruling Sui dynasty ended and the T'ang dynasty was founded. Within the same year the king of Koguryu also died, encouraging many to hope that a peaceful agreement between the two countries could be reached. Initially, all looked good as the three kingdoms sent peace envoys to the Chinese court. The emperor Kao-tsu accepted their offerings and for a time peace did reign. However, it was not long before the three kingdoms were back at each other's throats, fighting skirmish after skirmish. With first one side winning, then the other, the T'ang emperor watched with interest, intending to form an alliance with the eventual winner. But there was then no way of knowing which kingdom would emerge triumphant.

The Wise Queen

Of the three kings Chim-p'yung of Silla was the most peace-loving and philosophical. He had a daughter, Song-duk, who was renowned for her wisdom and love of the people. When her father died she ascended to the throne. The first woman to rule a Korean kingdom, she dedicated herself to improving the living standards of her people. By now the neighbouring kingdom of Pak-je had fallen from favour with the Chinese rulers because it had been dishonest with the Emperor. The third warring kingdom, Koguryu, had by now seen a bloodthirsty queen ascend to their throne.

China's Kao-tsu's problem was which ruler to side with. He knew that Queen Song-duk of Silla ruled with kindness and insight, rather than by the sword. But if he helped her fight the other two kingdoms he would have to provide her with a large army to support her small fighting force. But while Kao-tsu was struggling with his dilemma, the Queen Song-duk made up his mind for him. She impressed the Emperor by sending her best young warriors to Kao-tsu for training in the martial arts. She had instucted the warriors to be eager and willing to learn, but at the same time be humble and show great respect for the Chinese Emperor. Kao-tsu was very impressed with the Queen's approach, particularly when she later established her own martial arts school where the soldiers trained the general public. Song-duk even drew up a special code of ethics to combine honesty, bravery, loyalty and justice with martial skills so that her young warriors would be more than just fighting machines. This code was called the *hwarang-do* or 'way of flowering manhood'. The Queen named this weaponless martial art after the Emperor of China, who had taught it to her soldiers. The name given was *t'ang-shou* meaning 'Tang dynasty hand'.

The Hwarang

All the men of the hwarang were young, strong, and fit, the cream of Silla manhood. Apart from the regular military training they received, the hwarang learned the disciplines of mind and body from the Buddhist priests. They voluntarily exposed themselves to severe hardships in order to condition themselves so they would become like steel. Fighting, marching, training, all were done at treble the accepted normal pace until eventually this hwarang army became more than a match for any invader, no matter how outnumbered they were.

Before long the deeds of the hwarang became legendary, not only on the battlefields, but for the way they conducted their lives. They have often been compared with the samurai warriors of Japan. Gradually, after gaining victory after victory, the Korean peninsula became unified under the banner of the Silla Kingdom. The people, inspired by the feats of their elite fighting men, began to adopt the unarmed fighting principle of taekwon-do. So popular did this art become, that it was soon turned into a sport and was a regular feature at athletic competitions and festivals.

The Demise of Taekwon-do

Towards the end of the 10th century the Kingdom of Silla because of internal dissention, was overthrown, and the Kingdom of the Koryo dynasty was founded. The Western name Korea derives from this dynasty. Because this kingdom's survival still rested on maintaining a strong army, tae kyon or taekwon-do was openly and actively encouraged by the government. It eventually became compulsory for all young men, from age six upwards, to practise the art.

For 500 years compulsory training in taekwon-do remained on the statute books of the Koryo government. Then came an era of enlightenment, and anything related to military training was scorned. So the rot had set in for this ancient fighting art. Many of the trained Buddhist monks went up into the mountains to become recluses, but they kept the art alive. By the time of the Japanese occupation in 1909 the art had almost died out. The Japanese put the final nail in its coffin by forbidding the practice of any kind of martial discipline. The few remaining stalwarts who possessed the knowledge of taekwon-do emigrated to China and Japan, looking for work and to start new lives. No restrictions on unarmed martial arts training existed in those countries.

Because of this emigration, taekwon-do became influenced slightly by other forms of martial arts. When Korea was liberated in 1945 many Koreans returned to their homeland bringing with them the refined and improved taekwon-do.

Modern Taekwon-do Emerges

For five years after World War II, taekwon-do existed in Korea under various forms and titles. The advent of the Korean War brought a man named Choi Hong Hi onto the scene. Choi, a professional soldier, taught the old tae kyon systems to his men and was eventually promoted to general in the Korean army. Through his military liaison with foreign units, Choi spread the knowledge of his system until it became international. In 1954 Choi became head of the board concerned with the development of a unified martial art. His suggestion of the name taekwon-do for the national art of Korea was enthusiastically received and adopted.

The Art of Kicking

Taekwon-do's kicks have great destructive power, and utilize some unique techniques, although many other styles of martial arts employ similar kicks. But perfection cannot be achieved because other styles do not possess the knowledge of the important basic forms found only in taekwon-do. It is only when power, speed, and correct stance are blended that accuracy and maximum destructive force can be obtained.

The legs are the most powerful natural weapon that a human being possesses for the defence of his life. Taekwon-do bases its kicks on the bound-spring principle. Muscles and tendon, when subjected to excess tensile strain, lose their elastic power, much as a rubber band, once overstretched, either snaps or loses its resilience. So the object in applying a kick is to be like a coiled spring that is suddenly released. Because so much emphasis is placed upon kicking in taekwon-do, a special series of stretching exercises was devised. These enable an exponent to train so that he may extend his legs to the standard required.

The Korean Tiger Division

In today's modern army in South Korea they have a special unit called the Tiger Division. All the soldiers in that division are practising martial artists. No one may gain entry to this elite group unless he holds a black belt ranking, first dan or better. It would seem that history has gone full circle, and the Koreans are back to the days of the hwarang-do.

Hapkido

There is one system of Korean martial art that exists solely and strictly for self-defence, and that is hapkido.
The art is related to tae kyon, from where it takes its kicks and punches , but hapkido was truly formed from the marrying of aikido and tae kyon. In a self-defence situation, a hapkido practitioner would stand his ground and wait for the assault. As soon as the would-be attacker made his move a soft circular block would deflect the approaching blow. Then in a dazzling series of counter-offensive techniques involving spring kicks, back kicks, and roundhouse kicks, the hapkidoist would pound his attacker into the ground. So effective is this art that, during the conflict in Vietnam, United States Green Berets were taught the skills of hapkido.

Hapkido Principles

The main difference between aikido and hapkido lies in the redirecting of the attacker. The hapkido man counterattacks so strongly and swiftly with tremendous force that the punishing onslaught totally overwhelms his adversary. Whereas in aikido, the main principle is just to quell the attack, without due force. A hapkido man will never meet an attack head on. Instead, he will step to the side and deflect the blow before going in with a murderous counterattack, taking maximum advantage of his opponent's motion. Hapkido has more than 300 different major techniques in its system. And the permutations allow for a range of tens of thousands of possible responses.

Because hapkido is primarily for self-defence purposes, it does not cater for patterns, forms or *katas*, those imaginary shadow-boxing-type exercises seen in the other martial arts.

Extensive knowledge of pressure points and the body's vital areas are also scrupulously learnt, the sole concept being to avoid being harmed while trying to inflict as much damage as possible on the adversary. Similarities in the kicking techniques of hapkido can be identified time and again with taekwon-do.

Because strength is not a critical factor in the art, hapkido lends itself to people of all ages and both sexes. One of the world's foremost authorities on this art is Korean-born Bong Soo Han, who now resides in the West. The hapkido symbol is written the same way as aikido, but the Korean pronunciation turns it into hapkido.

Tang Soo Do

Another Korean martial art that is enjoying great popularity in the West is *tang soo do,* meaning 'way of the tang hand'. When it originated, more than 2000 years ago, it was known as soo bahk.

The present grandmaster of the art is Hwang Kee, who founded the world headquarters for tang soo do in Korea shortly after World War II. The academy is known as the Moo Duk Kwan and claims 20,000 member black belts world wide. Tang soo do at first sight looks very similar to Japanese or Okinawan karate. This, according to Hwang Kee, is because of the common Chinese ancestry of both arts.

The training hall where participants engage in their art is called a *dojang*. The training tunic or uniform is a *tobok*.

Hwarang-Do

The ancient warrior skills of hwarang-do arrived in the West from Korea in 1972. Two brothers from Seoul, Joo Bang and Joo Sang Lee, set up a school in the USA to spread the system worldwide. Students learn the four basic sections within the art. They are, the internal power, external power, weapon power, and mental power. The system has 365 kicks, one for every day of the year.

Special Powers

Because of hwarang-do's emphasis on mental power, advanced students receive instruction in mind control. This leads to the development of ESP and clairvoyance with the ultimate aim of acquiring a sixth sense. Even the subject of telepathy is studied in great detail. The student of hwarang-do learns to become one with the laws of the universe. He believes that these powers, and more, lie within the potential of every human being and can be developed through the proper training methods.

In order to achieve a spiritual balance, hwarang-do practitioners learn medicine and healing in great detail. They believe that anyone who has the capability of causing injury and death to another human being should also possess the facility to heal as well. In effect, an adept of the art can kill or cure. Students learn a special type of finger pressure technique similar to acupressure. By manipulating certain points of the human anatomy, a practitioner can revive and cure a sick person or, for that matter, a vanquished mugger. This method is known as 'royal family finger healing'.

Hwarang-Do Comes into the Open

Joo Bang Lee is the present grandmaster of the hwarang-do system. This title was accorded to him on the death of his own teacher, Suahm Dosa, in 1969. Joo Bang Lee became the 58th holder of the title, which has an unbroken lineage of 1,800 years. The Lee Brothers learnt their art in a Buddhist temple high in the mountains of Korea. After graduating in the system, they received permission to open up a school themselves.

This was the first time in modern history that hwarang-do had been taught outside the Buddhist monastery. The strict veils of secrecy had been swept aside and the art was open to all those who wished to learn it.

The Sul Sa

The sul sa was a secret sect within the confines of hwarang-do. In ancient times its members were regarded as being almost magical because of the very special feats they performed. These special agents, or spies, underwent the most severe martial arts training possible. A sul sa could be classed almost as a one-man army. The job of the sul sa was to spy on the opposing forces, or assassinate the top enemy generals. It was said of them, that they could dislocate their own joints at will, to slip out of the most complicated knots. They could scale the sheerest castle walls with ease, and actually walk on water using special boat-like shoes. Because of their techniques in camouflage it was thought that the sul sa could even make themselves invisible. All these things, combined with supreme empty hand and weapons techniques, made them invaluable to the forces of the hwarang.

Modern Day Sul Sa

Today, many of the secret skills of the sul sa are being taught to the world's elite fighting forces. One of the foremost authorities on the subject was the late Michael Enchanis, who learnt the art from his mentor, Joo Bang Lee. Enchanis, after his experiences in the Vietnam war with the 75th Ranger Battalion, began to wish for a martial art that could be geared for every encounter, no matter what it might be. He felt that although he had been given the best military training at the time, Western special forces units still had a lot to learn about jungle and guerrilla warfare.

Using the knowledge gained in the study of hwarang-do from Joo Bang Lee, Michael Enchanis developed a brand new concept of training that would allow soldiers and special service personnel to cope with any situation. After convincing military chiefs as to the effectiveness of the ancient sul sa methods adapted for modern warfare, he was given the go-ahead to teach selected men for a three-week training program. This unique course was conducted at Fort Bragg, North Carolina.

There, they learnt special unarmed combat methods, based upon the skills of hwarang-do. Included in the course was sentry stalking; defence against armed attack; mind control of the enemy, using advanced techniques of psychology; choking and neck-breaking; acupressure for self-healing; hypnosis for combat; and wilderness survival.

One of the most important aspects of modern sul sa training is teaching men to control their own thoughts as well as the thoughts of others. Meditation and some principles of Zen Buddhism are used. This is combined with an absolute positive attitude and the will to succeed. Controlling the thoughts of others is done by subtly using the power of suggestion and learning to talk in a relaxed manner, although there is a deadly intent in the mind of the user. The training experiment was a great success, and many thousands of service personnel have since followed it.

Unfortunately Michael Enchanis, the instigator of this blending of ancient martial arts skills with modern day warfare, was killed in Nicaragua in a helicopter accident, but the skills he taught live on.

Other Martial Arts of the World

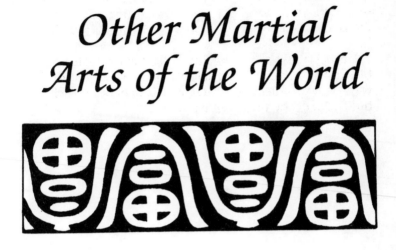

Martial Arts of the World

To know the outcome, look to the root.
Study the past to know the future.

Every country in Asia over the centuries had developed its own forms of fighting arts. By far the greatest influence on them all has been China. Nevertheless many nations have their own indigenous fighting skills, developed through many hundreds of years by trial and error, adversity and the continued fight for freedom.

Muay Thai

Wherever one may wander in the Orient among the many schools of fighting art one will not find a deadlier group of combatants than the kick boxers of Thailand. Many great masters in the martial arts accept that the Thai boxer is lethal because he is a professional and lives just to fight. Many people look upon *muay thai*, the correct term for Thai boxing, as a sport. This may be partly true, but the legacy of this 2000-year-old art lives on today in the hearts of the Thai people. One visit to Thailand will confirm this. Down any street one can see young children going through the rudiments of this ancient Siamese fighting art.

The old Kingdom of Siam, as Thailand was once known, has from ancient times always seen trouble from its neighbours. Occupying the Southeast Asian peninsula, it has Burma to the west, Laos to the north and east, and Cambodia to the south. Yet amazingly the so called 'land of the free' has resisted all attempts to conquer it. One can only put this down to the fierce fighting spirit of the people. Muay thai techniques have always been part of the military training system, which was greatly influenced by Chinese fighting methods in the beginning. It later underwent a marked change and developed independently, losing many of the Chinese boxing methods along the way. It is somewhat of a mystery how and why this happened, and for that matter why many of muay thai's special fighting techniques are not seen anywhere else outside Thailand.

The Tiger King

Because the Siamese people were combative by nature, the common folk picked up the military unarmed fighting methods and developed them into a sport, but they still retained all the lethal blows. Further skills were developed during the reign of King Pra Chao Sua, who was known as the 'Tiger King'. Every village staged its prize fights, with young and old, rich and poor all taking part. The king himself was a highly skilled boxer and was reputed to have trained with his soldiers six hours a day. He would often leave his palace disguised as a wandering peasant and enter boxing events, always defeating the local champions. The king would spend hours alone in his palace perfecting certain techniques, and then try them out in local contests. So skilled were some of his boxing strategies that even today they are still used and known as the Tiger King style.

The Greatest Fighter of Them All

Over the centuries the greatest of the muay thai fighters have become legendary. Stories are told of their battles and adventures to eager listening children by the village story teller. Perhaps the most famous of all Siamese fighters was Nai Khanom Dtom. He was a brilliant athlete and a strong courageous man, holding the title of the best fighter in all Siam. During the many wars that Siam had with her neighbour Burma, Nai Khanom Dtom was captured by Burmese soldiers. They had heard of his great fighting ability so they decided to pit him against 12 of Burma's top bando fighters (*bando* is the martial art of Burma, and similar in style to Thai boxing), and if he could defeat all 12, Nai Khanom Dtom would be allowed to go free.

So the next day in a stadium packed with thousands of people, Nai Khanom Dtom prepared to fight bare-handed against the cream of Burma's fighters. One by one they came at him, all out to kill him and become heroes themselves for defeating the greatest martial artist in Siam. As each fighter pitted his skills against the great Nai Khanom Dtom, he was instantly killed, being dispatched with lightning elbow strikes and murderous knee blows. As the day wore on, the great Siamese champion had slain nine of his adversaries. The spectators, who had been cheering for their own men, suddenly began to cheer for this magnificent fighter from Siam. They were full of admiration for the prisoner who had fought and killed nine men without rest or being wounded himself. By the end of the day 12 bodies lay in the dry dust of the stadium, and standing tall and undefeated was the great Nai Khanom

Dtom. The King of Burma had no alternative but to let him go free.

Today, many centuries after that event, Thai boxers honour him by dedicating one fight night each year to Nai Khanom Dtom.

No Rules or Regulations

In 1930 muay thai underwent a transformation. A number of rules and regulations were introduced including the wearing of boxing gloves and groin guards, and certain weight divisions were stipulated. Until that time, virtually anything was allowed in the ring. One favourite device used by the boxers was hemp rope bound around the fist to act as a form of glove. Then it was dipped in glue and rolled in finely ground glass. The effects of this adjunct in the ring were dramatic.

Deaths in the Ring

The elbow and the knee are probably the Thai boxer's deadliest weapons. It was because of uncontrolled elbow blows to the head, especially the temple, that most of the deaths occurred in the ring during fights. The knee attacks to the groin left many fighters with smashed testicles. Muay thai was known as a tough art. In order to survive at all, a fighter had to be quicker and stronger and more skilled than his opponent. Even in the small mountain villages deaths in the ring were common, right up until World War II. But new rules quickly put an end to the staggering death toll in the ring.

Growth of the Art Today

With the spread of contact sport among martial artists throughout the world, Thai boxing has burgeoned all over Asia. In Japan, Thai boxing has reached epic proportions in recent years. Nowadays the deadly elbow strike is banned, except in Thailand. Followers of many other martial disciplines will on most occasions refuse to fight a Thai boxer because they regard him as a complete fighting machine honed to proficiency through years of hard and intensive training. Those who dare to take up the challenge usually taste bitter defeat.

Training a Thai Boxer

As soon as a little Thai boy can walk he is introduced to kick boxing. Virtually 95 percent of all Thai youngsters begin boxing in earnest before they even learn how to read and write. Every village, town, and city has some form of boxing ring or stadium. If a youth shows any kind of promise in competition he is sent to one of the many special training camps scattered around the country. There the youngsters will eat, sleep, and live Thai boxing. The training regimen is very strict and life is hard, but a successful fighter can earn a lot of money during his time in the ring.

In the training of a boxer, much emphasis is placed upon stamina, for it is this energy that keeps a man moving fast enough and long enough to win the fight. To build up this stamina much roadwork is done. At the *prakong* or 'training camp', fighters run up to 10 miles a day. After a short rest, they plunge into the river and swim, forever building up endurance. From there they go onto the bags, and spend hours kicking away until their legs feel like lead. Then they undergo a unique series of stretching exercises. It is all this severe and intensive training that makes Thai boxers what they are. Because young fighters work so hard and tend to lead an austere and frugal existence, there is little danger of their gaining weight or getting fat in the wrong places. Most champion muay thai fighters look thin and undernourished, but underneath that exterior beats the heart of a lion with the strength and vitality to match.

Superstitions

As with many combatants through the ages, western or eastern, the wearing of talismans, or the use of charms, spells, and good luck pieces plays an important part in the gladiatorial make-up of a Thai boxer. They use these talismans for protection in the ring. They have an unshakable conviction that such items can transform them into invulnerable supermen. Muay thai fighters have a multitude of such amulets. Their faith is partly superstitious and partly religious. One superstition concerns the use of the *nan* leaf (pronounced 'whan'). A fighter puts this leaf in his mouth before a fight, usually under the tongue, in the belief that by doing so he gains protection against elbow and knee attacks. He believes that the leaf somehow makes his skin thick and, as a result he will not bleed or even get cut.

Another good luck ritual exercised by the fighters when entering the ring, is to place offerings in the form of flowers to the guardian spirit of the ring, to grant them victory over their opponent. The fighters also wear a cord called *kruang rang* tied around their upper arm. This usually conceals a miniature statue or figure of the lord Buddha. Other superstitions forbid women to enter the ring. Their presence allegedly radiates bad vibrations and brings bad luck to the fighters. But the establishment of women's Thai boxing leagues in recent years, has done much to dispel this particular belief.

The Religious Aspect of Muay Thai

Perhaps we in the West are not yet fully aware of the important way in which religion and the martial arts go hand in hand in the East. This dualism seems to be something of a contradiction in Western terms but it is no accident that the scientific principles of combat were, more often than not, formulated in monasteries and temples. Muay thai practitioners are devoutly religious, and their art is firmly rooted in Buddhism. In fact, many young fighters have served time as disciples in monasteries before going to the boxing camps.

Ram Muay: the Deadly Dance

Before any fighter begins to fight, he goes through a ritualistic dance known as *ram muay*. Every camp has its own form of this dance, and to the seasoned spectator it is quite possible to tell which camp the fighter has come from without knowing anything about him. The pre-fight ritual of ram muay also serves to tone up the fighter's muscles. Interestingly enough, within the dance lie all the basic moves of Thai boxing.

The boxing masters have their own ideas as to how this dance should be performed. When the fighter emerges from his corner to begin his ram muay it indicates to all present that he is showing great respect to the master who taught him his art. This little gesture of obeisance to the teacher is called *wai kruh*.

The fighter begins by bowing three times in the

direction of the camp he came from. This acknowledges the camp, his parents, and Buddha. The whole idea of the ritual is to try and psyche out his opponent and instil fear into him, implying that he has already beaten his man without a blow being struck. As the dance ends, the fighter walks back to his corner where his master is usually waiting on the other side of the ropes to whisper a special prayer of good luck to him. The prayer, strangely enough, is not uttered in the Thai language, but in Balinese. This blessing by his teacher is called 'the Buddha breath'. When finished, the master blows three times on the fighter's forehead. In many Eastern cultures the forehead is said to be the seat of the third eye, the mystical eye of knowledge and understanding.

The Monkon

When a Thai boxing student has undergone his first twelve months of training he attends a special ceremony known as Teacher's Day. On this day all new students who have been training for a year have to formally approach the master of the camp bearing either a white flower or a small gift of silver. He officially asks the master if he will accept him as a student, and requests permission to represent the boxing school in the ring. The master, usually seated and dressed in white, decides whether or not the student can join the ranks. If the master does accept him, he will present the student with his own *monkon*. This is the traditional headband worn by all Thai boxers. Very great reverence is shown to it, and it also denotes that the student now has a teacher and belongs to a camp. After the ceremony the student swears an oath of allegiance to belong to that particular camp forever.

A ring name is then awarded to each accepted student. This is decided according to personal characteristics. The surname is the name of the camp he belongs to and that is why so many of the boxers seem to have the same surname.

The Thai Boxing Tournament

Specification of the Thai boxing ring resemble those of international rings, together with a red corner and a blue corner. The weight categories are also similar to Western standards. Although officially fighters must be over 18, contestants as young as eight and nine years old fight for prize money in the rings. During all fights Thai music is played, with the tempo and volume varying to coincide with the action in the ring. Each bout consists of five three-minute rounds, with two minutes break between each round. A boxer may win by a knockout, a technical knockout, or a decision. Thai boxing has a stringent code of ethics, and high mental and physical discipline is required of the contestants. Today muay thai is almost completely a contest art, as is sumo wrestling. The rigorous training, effective techniques, high conduct of sportsmanship, and unsurpassed courage have commanded the respect of other martial artists. Their unbeaten record is impressive, and to date there is no evidence of a well-ranked Thai boxer having been knocked out by a martial artist from any other style.

Gambling and the Gangster Element in Muay Thai

Boxing in Thailand is big business with thousands of *baht* (Thai dollars) changing hands at every tournament. Like most Asian peoples, the Thais are great gamblers. This leads to criminal involvement in the sport. Thai gangsters often threaten the lives of the participants and many fights are rigged. At a modern tournament in a big city it is not uncommon for a fighter's manager or his seconds to escort him into the ring armed with a pistol. A few years ago a famous Thai boxer who now lives in Europe had a brush with the Thai underworld. He was told that he had to stop winning fights because the racketeers were losing money heavily on his continued wins. One particular evening he was approached and informed that if he didn't throw that night's fight and take a dive in the third round he would not be alive the following morning. The Thai boxer was a simple country lad who had made good and was on his way to becoming national champion of his country. He was fiercely proud and refused to accede to the gangsters.

So when he entered the ring for his fight, the young boxer went all out to win and in the second round he knocked his opponent out. He claimed the prize money and promptly left the ring. Later that night on his way home, two gangsters stepped out of the shadows and pumped three bullets into the brave boxer. Mercifully he survived the attack and within four months he was back in the ring. But he knew that his days must now be numbered so with discretion he left for Europe to teach the principles of muay thai there.

Krabi-Krabong: the Weapon Art of Thailand

Krabi-krabong is the revered art of Siamese sword and stick fighting. Its history is vague but it is believed to be more that 500 years old and stems from some form of army training. Fighting with the twin swords requires a great deal of skill. It takes a person nearly five years to learn all the basic techniques. A krabi-krabong match has no time limit and is truly a test of stamina and endurance. The bout ends only when the loser admits defeat and submits to his foe. Because the fighters wear no protective clothing or equipment, blood is often shed and injuries and torn garments are all quite normal. Cracked skulls, broken arms, legs and necks are also commonplace in these fights. As happened in kendo, the twin sword of krabi-krabong has today been replaced by hard wooden sticks. In a match, anything goes. If a weapon is lost or dropped the user can revert to judo-type throws or even kick and punch. The emphasis all the time is upon action.

The Burmese Art of Bando

Thailand's neighbour, Burma, has an art called *bando,* which closely resembles muay thai. It is not unreasonable to assume that because of the close historical association between these two countries, this sister art evolved from Thai boxing.

The general term for the Burmese martial arts is *thaing,* which means self-defence by both armed and unarmed methods. Bando is actually boxing by any other name.

Bando Techniques

Bando's techniques include the usual blocking and striking methods employed by many martial arts. But within the system there are also to be found grappling and locking techniques. After a student has learned the basic postures, which are based on 12 animals, similar to that of many kung fu styles, he then learns to develop his techniques by sparring with other students. The roundhouse kick is delivered with the shin, just like in Thai boxing.

Bando in the West

The bando system was introduced into the West in the early 1960s by a Burmese doctor named Maung Gyi. Even in modern times, the art of Bando is still rarely seen outside of Burma. Because the bando system is so versatile and has both a hard and soft subdivision, men and women can train in the various forms with little difficulty. Each of the animal styles in bando is specifically suited to people of certain strength, size, speed, and reactions. Once the instructor has determined a student's physical make up he can introduce him or her to the animal style that best suits them.

The Tiger of Bando

The tiger system of bando trains its adepts to behave like the animal itself. A fighting attitude is cultivated to characterize ferocious aggression, and this can be converted into a raging attack. The weapons of the tiger are its claws and jaws, so a student tries to emulate the animal by turning his fingers and thumb into claws for ripping and gouging the enemy. Attacks are usually directed towards the throat, neck, and face.

Way of the Disciplined

Bando means 'way of the disciplined'. Although practised for hundred of years in Burma it only came to prominence after a revival of national arts and warrior skills by the Japanese in 1941. There are 12 animals in the system, but the symbol of all the bando systems is the black panther. This animal was chosen for its fighting versatility.

Within the cobra techniques of bando lie all the lightning fast, paralysing nerve strikes. The cobra is considered to be the most difficult of all the bando animal systems to learn. Bando is a complete martial art, and is geared like most other Asian skills to develop the practitioner's inner qualities of tranquillity and humility as well as building up his physique and fighting prowess.

Banshay

The Burmese form of weapon arts are known as *banshay*. The main weapons are the short sword, staff, and spear. These all have sophisticated schools of technique. The Burmese swordsmen unlike their Japanese counterparts, consider it bad form to kill or even injure an opponent. Their objective is merely to disarm an attacker without hurting him. Included within these weapon skills is also the bow-and-arrow.

The Indonesian Art of Pentjak-silat

The national defence form of Indonesia is called pentjak-silat. It developed on the island of Sumatra sometime in the seventh century. Then over the years, by means of island-hopping from Sumatra to Java, and thence to Indonesia, the art influenced all who came into contact with it along the way. Ending up in Indonesia, it was further refined and developed. Today there are more than

150 distinct recorded styles of pentjak-silat. *Pentjak-silat* means 'to fight using skilled and specialized body movements'. The art encompasses armed and unarmed techniques. Because of its light and graceful movements it has often been classified as a dance but used against an enemy there is no doubt that it can be a deadly fighting art. When fighting, both arms are always in motion, as in a dance, but the eyes are focused on the opponent all the time. The extremely rapid movement of the pentjak-silat fighter tend to bemuse an opponent and the attack comes without warning. The fighter suddenly erupts into punches and kicks, striking at vital parts of the body before sweeping the opponent to the ground to finish him off.

The Legend of Silat

Legend ascribes the origin of pentjak-silat to a woman. Long ago in Sumatra a woman was sent down to the stream by her husband to fetch water. As she stooped to fill the bucket from the stream, she noticed a tiger attacking a huge bird. Fascinated, she watched the battle for several hours until finally both animals died. Getting up to leave, she was suddenly confronted by her angry husband who had come down to the stream to see why his wife was taking so long fetching the water. The husband hit out at her in temper, but she evaded him easily, using the methods of the two animals she had just been watching. Her amazed husband stared back in disbelief as his every blow was either blocked or neutralized. Later on the wife taught her husband what she had learned, and pentjak-silat as an art was launched. To back up that old story, Sumatrans point out that there are still women today who are experts in the art.

The Muslim Tradition

Because pentjak-silat thrived in Islamic Sumatra, it has often been erroneously regarded as a strictly Muslim art, but this is not true, although most of its practitioners are Muslims. Because of its religious background, pentjak-silat has a profound philosophy behind it. All silat is influenced by the Koran, and the exponents of pentjak-silat strive through their martial art to seek *ihan* or 'spiritual inspiration'.

The Art as a Combat Form

Pentjak-silat used for combat training is referred to as *gayong* or *buah silat*. This kind of silat is a strange combination of delicate movement and forceful action. Combat silat dispenses with all that is not immediately related to practical results in hand-to-hand fighting. Every adept learns to protect himself from both armed and unarmed assailants, while he himself may be either armed or unarmed. As a result all training for combat silat involves the study of a wide range of weapons.

No Wages for the Teacher

Traditionally, the *guru* or 'teacher' of pentjak-silat accepted no payment from his pupils. He accepted just a token donation to keep him in clothes. The guru's skill existed only to be used to teach worthy disciples, and could not be used for profit. When a student wished to train in the art he was required to bring with him five offerings for the guru: a chicken, so that the blood from it could be spread on the training ground as a symbolic substitute for the student's own blood; a roll of white cloth for wrapping his body in, should the student die during training; a knife, to symbolize the student's sharpness; tobacco, so that the teacher could smoke during his rest period; and finally, a little money to replace the teacher's clothes, should they be ripped in practice.

Once accepted, the disciple swore an oath on the Koran, and became a blood brother to all the other students.

The Harimau Style

The most popular style of silat in Sumatra is called *harimau*, and resembles the antics of a tiger. Because of the damp conditions in the area where this particular style originated a normal upright stance and movement were discarded in favor of ground-hugging movements. A combatant crouches close to the ground and inches his body forwards until he is within striking range. This style requires great strength and flexibility in the hips and legs.

Malaysian Bersilat

Malaysian bersilat is derived from Indonesian pentjak-silat which it resembles. But in spite of this, it is technically different in many ways. The name *bersilat* means 'to do, by fighting'. The art is divided into two styles. One is a dance form that is displayed on public holidays. This has lost much of its fight realism and is practised merely for the grace and poise it develops. The other style is known as *buah* and this is a hard, effective combat method that is never publicly seen. Buah, the combat side of bersilat, contains techniques which make considerable use of the legs and looks quite acrobatic in nature. The secrecy that surrounds this art ensures that only the most dedicated and select student know its innermost mysteries. The vows they take forbid them to divulge anything that they learn.

Modern Bersilat

In Malaysia, bersilat training is considered to be a perfect physical exercise and a sport. It is taught in schools and colleges throughout the peninsula. This modern version of the art has nothing like the combative value its ancestor had, and is really quite diluted. It is only in remote areas and the outer islands that the true bersilat still exists, and that is not open to the eyes of anyone except the true devotee.

Capoiera: the Slave Art of Brazil

One of the most overlooked martial arts in the world is that of Brazil's capoiera. This art was born out of slavery, in personal defence of cruelty and persecution. Capoiera was invented by the blacks to fight the vicious slave owners and had its most terrifying results in the slave uprisings. For centuries, the blacks kept their art alive under a sworn oath of secrecy. The authorities refused to recognize that such an art ever existed, because if they did, it would attest to the ability of blacks to fight back, thus causing further unrest and insurrection.

Many of the movements are highly acrobatic in application. Some of the foot striking techniques are delivered as the fighter performs a cartwheel on his hands. It is believed that the origins of the art lie in certain African folk dances and that the choreography was altered and adapted to suit the purposes of self-defence. It was through these dances that the slaves managed to hide the lethal aspects of this martial art from the landowners.

Native Art Form

In 1965 the Brazilian government recognized capoiera as a native art form and consequently accepted it as a sport, albeit somewhat reluctantly. One of the greatest teachers of capoiera was Master Bimba who, aided by an anthropologist named Benjamin Muniz, pieced together the various movements of the capoiera dance-cum-martial art and formulated it into a type of long kata to aid students in their instruction. For many reasons the government kept a close watch on its modern development because official thinking always identified the art with rebellion and with the anti-social elements of Brazilian society.

The Outlawed Dance

Capoiera had been outlawed for over 200 years and its re-introduction in modern times as part of the native cultural heritage was met with fierce opposition.

In capoiera the emphasis is on muscular strength combined with joint flexibility and rapid movement. Making use of very fast body reaction the capoiera fighter can deliver a blow with his feet that could smash a man's internal organs. In a fraction of a second he flips his body over, in a type of handstand and delivers with tremendous force and accuracy a double foot blow to the aggressor's body that could well nigh cut him in two.

Without a doubt a capoiera man's feet are his deadliest weapons. He trains to kick as most martial artists train to punch. It has been said of capoiera, that it is one of the dirtiest formalized fighting styles known.

Amazing Stories

As with most martial arts, legends abound. Stories circulate of how in the old days capoiera fighters used to tape knives and razors to their bare feet before entering a fight. In Rio de Janeiro police tried to arrest a capoiera man who had become drunk. Apparently this master of the art despatched nearly two dozen of them before he was finally subdued by force of the gun. On another occasion a 72 year old capoiera master was accosted in the street by a gang of sailors. Eye witness accounts state that they had barely knocked him to the ground when the old man suddenly sprang into action. His feet scythed into the attackers, cutting them down like ninepins. When the police arrived, the old man had disappeared, leaving in his wake twelve sailors in desperate need of hospitalization.

Capoiera is not a complicated martial art. It has little more than 72 defined separate movements. Many of its techniques have colourful titles such as 'tail of the dragon fish', 'daddy's scissors' and 'banana plant'. Just like martial arts the world over, capoiera had one prime function; it was invented to kill.

Filipino Kali

Records dating back to 750 AD indicate that the ancient peoples of the Philippines had developed a highly specialized form of weapon fighting. *Kali* comes from a Malay word meaning 'bladed weapon'. In learning this art, one starts by learning about the weapon first and the empty-hand method last. The weapon concerned is the machete-like knife known as the *bola*. With this in one hand and dagger in the other, the kali practitioner was an awesome sight in battle, as Ferdinand Magellan found out when he invaded the island of Cebu in 1521. Even though the attacking Spaniard had far superior weapons, they were defeated by natives bearing knives and sticks.

Arnis de Mano

Although kali was the ancient martial art of the Philippines, it is the Spanish term *arnis de mano*, 'harness of the hand', that describes the self-defence system of the Philippines. This art in the main uses twin sticks and bladed weapons. Arnis also goes under another name, *escrima* which means 'skirmish' in Spanish. By whatever name it goes under, it is one of the deadliest fighting arts of the Orient.

Imperial Invaders

When the Spanish invaded the Philippines, they had a hard time imposing their rule on the inhabitants and were constantly attacked by razor-sharp bolos, twin sticks, and daggers. It was only through the use of firearms that the invaders could bring about any semblance of order. When finally Spanish rule was firmly established the conquerors set about banning the learning and teaching of arnis de mano. The carrying of the bolo was also forbidden in an attempt to minimize the heavy death toll among the occupying troops. The art of escrima or arnis de mano went underground, as did karate in Okinawa when the occupying Japanese issued similar edicts. The art eventually re-emerged and went unnoticed by the Spanish because it had been set to music and resembled a dance.

Because the art was learned in secret (some classes were even taught by moonlight), and because many of the hundreds of islands were widely separated and hosted different languages, many styles grew up independently of each other. Much to their dismay, the Spanish found themselves under constant harassment from the Morro tribesmen's guerrilla tactics. These tactics persisted on and off for nearly three hundred years of Spanish colonization.

When the United States won the Spanish-American War the Filipinos thought they would get self-rule. But the islands were too strategically valuable, so Americans merely replaced the Spaniards. Although the Philippines now had a new benevolent master, the fierce Morro natives would not be subjugated. Their ferocious fighting techniques, using twin sticks and bolo knives, exacted a deadly toll of the lives of the American marines occupying the islands.

To try and put an end to the losses suffered by his troops, General Pershing issued a special leather neck-covering for his men. This protected them from having their throats cut and helped to lower the terrifying casualty rate. This is why the US marines are known the world over as 'leathernecks'.

During World War II it was the Japanese who felt the sting of the Filipino martial arts. The tribesmen alongside American service personnel fought with their ancient blades and twin sticks to defeat the Japanese occupying forces. After the war, many Filipinos emigrated to the United States. Needless to say, their arnis de mano went with them. Most of the immigrants went to Hawaii and California.

Escrima Tactics

A tactic in escrima called *retirada,* or 'retreating style', is designed for encounters where the fighter has time and room to keep backing away in order to study his opponent's movements. When a fighter is forced to make a stand, the opposite tactic is used – the *fondo fuerte,* or 'non-retreating style'. All the footwork in escrima works on the lines of a triangle. The triangular footwork comes into its own when a person is attacked with his back to the wall with no prospects of moving anywhere. This doesn't make the slightest difference to an escrimador because a triangle fits into a corner perfectly. In other words, he is never trapped because he is used to working on the triangular pattern.

The Song of the Butterfly

Most students of escrima and kali somewhere along the way in their training learn the use of a little knife known as the *balisong,* or 'butterfly knife'. This Filipino knife dates back more than a thousand years. Legend has it that a great Filipino warrior trained in the martial art of kali and armed solely with this small razor-sharp folding knife, took on in mortal combat 29 enemy warriors – and killed them all. The Spanish word for the blade is *veintinueve,* which means 'twenty-nine' and it commemorates that great feat. The knife actually took its name from a *barrio* in the Philippines called Balisung. *Bali* means 'to break', and *sung* means 'horn'. The people of that town are said to have been the first to produce the broken horn knife.

This was first introduced into the States by the early immigrant farm workers, and later by returning GIs who brought them home as war souvenirs. Because of the click-click noise made by the knife when it is flicked open, second-generation Filipino American children likened the sound to that of a butterfly rubbing its wings. As a result, it became known as the butterfly knife. Another version of the name's origin and perhaps a little more believable than listening to the sound of a butterfly rubbing its wings together, is that when the knife is half-open it resembles a butterfly in flight.

The Balisong Today

The butterfly knife has twin handles that when folded completely envelop the blade, thus eliminating the need for a sheath. The knife is opened by a flick of the wrist and the handles revolve in opposite directions to be caught in the user's hand and held together for a solid grip. The martial arts world took to this weapon immediately. Today the knife has been patented by Les de Asis and the name Balisong has been officially registered.

The Martial Arts of India

Kalaripayit

In southern India, in the province of Kerala, an art called *kalaripayit* is practised. Kalaripayit means 'battlefield training'. A *kalari* is the place where the participants practise and is the equivalent of a karate dojo. There are two distinct styles: the northern style, which is very hard and is practised by the Nayers who are the warrior caste, and the southern style, which is dominated by the Tamils. Because the country is so vast, the two styles are quite noticeably different.

In the north the kalaripayit is tremendously energetic. Participants kick about eight feet into the air with their legs vertical. They do exercises in which one minute the leg is absolutely vertical, right up in the air, and the next minute comes crashing down into a complete splits. The kalari measures exactly 21 ft by 42 ft. There is endless salutation and bowing to gods and altars. In the south, the style is rugged and the stances are much shorter. It has a crude look to it, being less supple and energetic.

Origins

The martial art of kalaripayit is based on a series of ancient documents called *sastras*. These are secret writings passed on through the ages and written on palm scrolls. They list 108 vital points on the body which, if struck, will cause death. The system is very similar to Japanese atemi. This dark side of the art is termed *marma-adi* and it is taught only to the most advanced students. A peculiar aspect of the northern style is that all practice is conducted at night and in secret.

The Evil Eye

Because of its advanced techniques marma-adi has become a separate branch of the art of kalaripayit. A master of marma-adi does not teach exercises or forms, he concentrates only teaching the vital points and resuscitation techniques. A certain amount of fear has grown among villages through the ages about the metaphysical powers of these masters. A sort of witchdoctor image has been conjured up, and it is said that if someone offends a marma-adi master, he only has to look that person straight in the eye in order to kill him, lending a bizarre truth to the old saying, 'if looks could kill'. All masters of kalaripayit are traditional doctors in their own right.

The Village Art

Kalaripayit is still mostly a village art, but on a huge scale. There are least 500 schools practising in southern India alone. The art was practised in secret under the British, during their colonization of India in the last century and, as far as is known, kalaripayit is purely indigenous to India. Students of the art are not allowed to train in it before they have undergone a month of special massage to get their bodies into a receptive state. The only type of uniform worn is a pelvic girdle that acts like a truss and supports the groin. This bandage-like contraption measures 40 feet in length, and is applied to the body by first tying the end round a tree trunk. Then the students wind themselves up in it like a cocoon.

The art on the whole is very tough. Throws are practised on solid stone floors. It also includes a very fast form of shadow boxing. On the soft side, it involves lots of throws and locks. Kalaripayit also has a complex weapons system that includes hundreds of disarming techniques, as well as all combinations of unarmed combat. In both styles there are four main categories, beginning with unarmed techniques, then training with bamboo twin sticks, followed by knives, spears, and swords. It ends with learning the vital secrets of the mystical marma-adi.

Kalaripayit is riddled with religious overtones – so much so that on occasions when there have been no students the kalari has been turned into a temple, or a sacred lamp is lit every day and it is just left. A kalari is never pulled down. Students of the art must be obedient, they must respect Kali, the goddess of war, and always show proper respect to their master.

The Cult of Thuggee

During the latter part of the nineteenth century in India, there arose a group or cult of fanatics who practised the killer art of *thuggee*. These people were rebelling against the British. At one time they had all been practitioners of kalaripayit, and were masters of marmi-adi. To create havoc and fear amongst the British, they would steal into the British camps and barracks at dead of night and strangle soldiers by means of a silken scarf with a rupee coin encased within its folds. Death came quickly and silently, as the solid coin pressed against the victim's throat. These Indian fanatics claimed their goddess Kali had ordered them to do this in order to clear the British from India. The word 'thug' is derived from these ancient killers of Bombay, where the strongest thuggee sects existed. To Western eyes these methods may seem a little drastic – a misuse of the martial arts, perhaps. But to the followers of the cult, they were only doing what seemed natural to them – to rid their land of the forces of occupation by every possible means.

The Weapons of the Martial Artist

The Weapons of the Martial Artist

The assimilation of learning is called knowledge, and the proper use of that knowledge is called wisdom.

In the previous chapters we have learnt about many forms of empty hand styles and techniques. But not all martial arts are specifically empty hand ones. Some of them have become popular because of the weapon at the core of the system. These ancient tools of warfare serve the modern martial artist in his quest to gain mastery over himself and his art. Some of these latter-day instruments of war, to Western eyes, look rather curious. But in the hands of an expert, simple farming implements become lethal weapons.

The Sai

The sai or horn of death is today a weapon very much promoted by the karate movement. Traditionally Okinawa was the home of this weapon but it is also found throughout Southeast Asia, from India to the Philippines. It is a short-range weapon much resembling a trident, usually made of iron, and measuring 15 to 20 inches long.

Although looking like a very short sword, the tip is actually blunt. About one-third of the way down the shaft, two opposing prongs or tines are used as a handle to grip the weapon with. The sai, usually used in pairs, was capable of killing or maiming an enemy with a blow to the back of the neck, or a thrust to the throat or at the eyes. The butt or pommel of the sai was often used for striking at nerve points or at the temple. There are only two basic ways of gripping the sai – one is to hold it with the blade point outward, the other is with the blade pointing inward.

The Sai in Japan

The sai requires rigid training and great skill to manipulate it. When it was first introduced to Japan, it was adopted by the police force and used as a sort of iron truncheon. The Japanese police found it very effective in blocking the thrusts of the samurai's razor-sharp blades. During arrests it was used against criminals' pressure points in order to subdue them. Later, the Japanese altered the shape of the sai by losing one of the prongs. They then renamed it the jutte. This weapon was used by the police for a considerable time, until it was dropped in favour of the gun.

The Sai in Karate

It is said that the Brahmic god Indra, who was the guardian of holy places, especially temples, carried a crude version of what appeared to be a sai. Its use spread across Asia in one form or another. In Indonesia it is known as the tjabang, in China they call it the titkio. But this ancient weapon has finally found its acknowledged home in karate. One of the leading practitioners of the sai in the United States is the Japanese master, Fumio Demura.

Today, when the sai are used by karateka, they are made from tempered steel instead of iron. Although no longer used as a weapon in the strictest terms, a karateka wielding them in performance of the special sai kata known as *jigen* during a tournament demonstration makes a dazzling sight. His wrists and hands flick through the difficult movements with amazing dexterity.

A recent version of this weapon is the telescopic sai. This is a series of tubes within tubes, all metal. When flicked downwards by the wrist, it is transformed into a foot-long steel truncheon. This weapon is becoming increasingly popular as a form of protection against muggers.

The Nunchaku

The nunchaku was originally used as an agricultural tool to flail rice, but it was later developed on the island of Okinawa as a weapon during the Japanese occupation. Here again is a weapon that was thought to be purely indigenous to Okinawa, but in fact the nunchaku is to be seen all over Asia. It consists of two equal lengths of hardwood held together at the top by a cord or chain. The pieces of wood are about 12 to 15 inches long. The simple look of the apparatus disguises a truly awesome weapon. The nunchaku can be used to block or parry, or it can be swung with terrible force to deliver smashing blows at any assailant from long range. The cord that holds it together is used for choking.

The Springing Tiger

In present day martial arts no weapon has earned for itself more notoriety than the nunchaku. The *chuks* as they are sometimes called, are considered by the police and courts to be offensive weapons. A first glance two pieces of wood strung together by a length of cord may not look too fearsome a weapon, but in the hands of a skilled practitioner the nunchaku can be likened to an unleashed tiger springing into action and leaving carnage in its wake. It has been said that a pair of nunchaku used by an expert can keep several men at bay simultaneously.

When the nunchaku is in motion it is nearly impossible to grab it and take it away from the person wielding it. Blocks can be delivered in two places at the same time. It is a weapon that can be used at a distance and also at close quarters. This simple farming implement, once used for threshing grain by the people of Okinawa, has been developed and refined to become an awesome street weapon of the twentieth century. But there are two facets to this ancient weapon. Apart from being an instant injury implement, the nunchaku in the hands of a serious and dedicated karateka can be a source of inspiration for kata, and a dynamic tool for improving the martial artist's training regimen. Interestingly enough, when the nunchaku are used by an untrained person, they usually cause more harm to the wielder than to the attacker.

The early nunchaku was held together by rope plaited and braided from horse tails. It was a weapon that was easy to conceal and yet with a flick of the wrist it could be drawn out and used with deadly efficiency. Its construction was simple. It is fairly safe to assume that the early development of the nunchaku both as an agricultural implement and a weapon originated in China. Variants of it are seen in the Philippines, where it is known by the name of *tabok-toyok*, in Vietnam, Laos, Cambodia, and Malaysia.

Like the sai, the nunchaku was adopted primarily by students of karate. The karate man who had already developed agility, found the use of nunchaku in training extremely effective. The fast moves and quick thinking required with the use of this weapon add a bonus to martial arts training in general.

The Tonfa

The tonfa, sometimes called the *tui-fa*, was originally the handle used to turn a manually operated millstone. It had a shaft about 20 inches in length, with a grip attached to it about one-fourth of the way down. It was used as a weapon by gripping the handle, so that the shorter end extended past the knuckles. The longer end swung out freely from under the arm to hit its target. As with the sai, the tonfa can be used either singly or in pairs. It is made of white oak and weighs about 1 1/4 pounds. In martial arts circles it is only karate people who use this weapon. In the old days in Okinawa, students had to be third dan black belts or better, before they were allowed to train with it.

Modern Use of the Tonfa

During the late 1960s, when karateka began to adopt the tonfa as part of their training curriculum, law enforcement agencies began to take notice of this simple oriental weapon. A deputy sheriff by the name of Lon Anderson recalled an incident he had seen when serving in

Okinawa. He had witnessed a native policeman, virtually single-handed, put down a minor village riot. The policeman had gone into the thick of the mob whirling a pair of tonfa sticks. Striking out left and right at legs and arms, he quickly quelled the riot. Anderson thought that if that could be done in the Orient, the same could be done in the West. He adapted this ancient budo weapon into a single stick baton with a short arm protruding. In fact, an almost exact replica of the original. Today police forces all around the world use this Okinawan peasants' rice mill handle, as an efficient weapon.

The Kubotan

A scaled-down version of the tonfa available for civilian use is a little weapon known as the *kubotan.* The kubotan was invented by a Japanese sensei and weapons expert named Takayuki Kubota. It is a 2 1/2 inch cylindrical piece of solid plastic that is often disguised as a key ring. When applied in arm and joint locks, or at a nerve points it produces immediate excruciating pain. Sensei Kubota developed a special series of self-defence techniques to accompany the use of this weapon.

The Kama

The *kama* is a short sickle with a hardwood handle. At first glance it looks much like the kind of sickle that has been used for centuries in both eastern and western farming cultures. The tool is used for harvesting rice or cutting hay. But to the farmers of Okinawa it proved to be a valuable defence aid when the Japanese banned all weapons.

Farmers took their kamas, sharpened them to a razor's edge, then developed a series of defence measures by using the kama in pairs. Many a samurai has fallen foul of twin kamas when picking on a seemingly defenceless peasant. Today, as with a lot of these ancient weapons, they have found new life in the modern martial arts, only now they are made entirely of wood, even the blade.

Kusarigama

Man's ingenuity for defending himself knows no bounds, adaptability being the byword. The kama or common sickle was upgraded by the Japanese peasant to become a formidable weapon known as the *kusarigama* or swirling chain of death. This was a tool that could be used to challenge a sword-wielding samurai on his own terms. Basically, the kusarigama was a sickle with a length of chain between four and 15 feet long, with one end attached to the handle and the other fixed to a heavy steel ball. The ball measured about two inches in diameter. The idea was to whirl the ball and chain around a swordsman's arms and thus to ensnare him. This made it possible for the peasant to move in close and decapitate him with the kama. The action was similar to that of the *bolas*, used by the South American gaucho.

Sealed in Blood

The weapon came into being around the mid-1500s in Japan. It was adopted by the martial arts fraternities of the day, but was quickly dropped because of the extreme difficulty of its use. One school, however, retained it and expanded its techniques in use to such an extent that within 50 years a kusarigama could be used effectively against a samurai armed with twin swords. Students flocked to the school to learn the use of this weird and wonderful weapon, but acceptance was very strict because a novice student had to sacrifice many things in order to join. He had to pledge secrecy. He was not allowed to drink alcohol, nor when proficient at a later date was he allowed to open his own school. He must never argue with other school members, nor think or speak badly of his master. If knowledge of kusarigama techniques ever leaked out, it could be a matter of life and death, because an enemy could then develop counter-techniques. When a student had sworn to uphold this strict code of secrecy he was expected to seal a document with his own blood. This was performed by pricking the second knuckle on the student's left hand. If after this a student ever disclosed any of the school's secrets, he would be put to death in a very painful way.

Kwan Do

In the Chinese weapons systems, the traditional kwan do is surely the most impressive. The weapon is a curved blade between 18 and 24 inches long. It is mounted on the top of a five foot staff, with a metal point fitted to the bottom end. Legend states that it was invented by a Chinese general named Kwan Yu. General Kwan is often regarded as the patron saint of the Chinese martial arts because of his virtuous life and military skill. The original kwan do was said to weigh in the region of 120 pounds, and from all accounts was a mighty weapon. The kwan do is a long-range weapon.

Bring Me the Head of Hua Hsiung

General Kwan spent his life performing great deeds. On one occasion he presented himself in front of a powerful king who was having trouble with a mighty warrior called Hua Hsiung. Hua Hsiung had already killed two of the greatest fighters in the kingdom. General Kwan offered his services to the king, stating that if he failed to kill the rebel Hua Hsiung, he would offer his own head in exchange. Then grabbing his powerful weapon he rode off to engage the rebel chief in battle. A short time later General Kwan returned and threw the rebel leader's head at the feet of the king.

Today the kwan do can be seen in most kung fu schools, where its use in training develops the martial spirit.

The Samurai Sword

The sword or *katana* was the basic weapon of the samurai class. Before 700 AD, the blades were straight, but after that time they became curved in design and have remained so ever since. Making the sword was an art in itself, and once finished, the product was of the highest quality. The sword, like the cowboy's six-shooter, was with the owner at all times. There is no other country in the world where the sword has received so much honour and renown as in Japan. It became known as the very soul of the warrior class. All samurais carried two swords, one long, one short.

Testing the Cut

When not fighting, warriors would test their swords and cutting skills by a method known as *tameshigiri*, which required the use of corpses of decapitated criminals. The corpses were used either singly or in groups. By these methods the samurai developed many diversified cutting styles. They would continually chop at the corpses until they had been reduced to pieces the size of a man's hand. Most samurai would practise up to 3000 cuts a day, just to keep themselves up to scratch. If another warrior happened to brush past a samurai and accidently touched his sword, he would be instantly challenged. If the offender were a common peasant, he would have been instantly struck down and killed. This was permissible right up until 1876. Then an edict was passed forbidding the samurai to wear his traditional twin swords.

Chinese Swords and Other Weapons

Wu Shu Jien

The *wu shu jien* or *gim* is China's double-edged sword with a straight blade. Today this weapon is in constant use with the practitioners of tai chi chuan. They use it as an extension of their art. It is a beautiful weapon that has a long coloured tassel hanging from its hilt. This was always removed before any actual fighting began.

The Tiger Fork

The tiger fork, or trident, is a long spearlike weapon used originally to kill tigers in southern China. It eventually became a martial arts weapon and can often be seen accompanying lion dance groups when they perform their celebration ritual.

Butterfly Knives

The short, wide-bladed butterfly knives are seen in many kung fu styles. These should not be confused with the Filipino balisong, which is quite different. The *darn do* butterfly knives are one of the only two weapons used in the kung fu system of wing chun although choy lee fut has a similar weapon. Its popularity was probably due to the fact that crowded urban conditions made such a compact weapon desirable.

The Bo Staff

The *bo* staff, also known as a cudgel in China, really needs no introduction at all. This weapon can be seen in cultures the world over, although asiatic peoples put much more emphasis on its use than westerners ever did.

The Iron Fan

A very popular weapon in the Chinese schools of martial

arts was the iron fan. As a weapon, the fan was short and very convenient. It was carried daily for cooling purposes, but besides fanning the breeze, it could be used to kill an enemy. As a result, its possessor was perpetually armed. The fan was constructed very like the standard paper one except that the paper was glued to iron strips instead of bamboo. It was used for stabbing, lifting, and plucking. The striking power was generated from the wrists. Experts in its use could, if the occasion required, splay the fan out, and hurl it at an enemy to knock his head right off.

Conclusion

Many other weapons and unarmed arts that we have not mentioned exist in the world today. These include the sambo (now known as sombo) wrestlers of the Balkans, the Greco-Roman wrestlers, and the quarterstaff fighters of medieval Britain. The list is almost endless, country by country.

The changing face of the martial arts in recent years has led many students away from the traditional ways in search of something different. The tried and tested oriental training methods have been re-examined by the logical western mind in an effort to revamp certain elements of the martial disciplines, especially in the areas of coaching. Some schools of thought firmly believe that the Japanese and Chinese hold over western practice of the martial disciplines is fast in decline. In their place is a formalized fighting system which takes the best elements from a wide variety of sources in the search for the perfect martial arts system. This amalgamation of different styles, is termed 'eclectic'. Some of these new systems have caught on in a big way and are very successful. Others have burst onto the scene and then vanished just as quickly leaving no trace.

It seems certain that over the coming years more eclectic styles and systems will be introduced, each one purporting to outdo the other. Meanwhile, the future of self-defence techniques is guaranteed by the constant growth of urban violence which sadly seems to be a very prominent feature of life today. The eclectic systems that we see today differ in one very important respect from their ancient predecessors, in that they are devoid of any underlying philosophy or principles. It is perhaps at this point one wonders how long the traditional eastern martial arts would have lasted if they too had been nothing more than just fighting techniques. Two thousand years ago, the indigenous martial arts systems provided a vital answer to our quest for a life larger and more meaningful than one in which the fight for survival seemed to originate. The training they undertook in the various martial systems and the philosophies and ideals that were built as underlying factors in these systems, gave people broader horizons with the insight to believe that the practice of martial arts is more than just about fighting, it is about living life to the full.

Of one thing we can be certain, warfare and fighting in general have progressed at terrifying speed. In contrast with the early days of the martial arts, when they were first developing, modern technology has changed weaponry out of all recognition. But thanks to a dedicated band of martial arts practitioners in the Orient, a valuable legacy of fighting styles has been handed down and preserved for us to practise and appreciate in the twentieth century.

'Life is written on a great sheet called time, and once written is gone forever' (Old Chinese Proverb).

Glossary

Glossary

Acupuncture Ancient Chinese system of healing involving the insertion of needles at certain key points in the body to stimulate nerve impulses.

Aikido Japanese martial art of which there are many styles. The most popular is Ueshiba, named after its founder, Morihei Ueshiba.

Arnis de mano Filipino martial art involving twin short hard wooden sticks.

Atemi Japanese art of attacking and striking the vital points of the body.

Balisong Butterfly knife, small switchblade-type knife opened by a downward wrist action. Used in the Philippines with deadly efficiency.

Bando Burmese boxing method.

Bersilat Malayan martial art also practised in Indonesia and Sumatra. Present day emphasis is more on the sporting form.

Black Belt The black belt indicates that the student has reached a level of proficiency in certain martial arts, in order to teach himself.

Bodhidharma Indian monk also known as Ta-Mo, the legendary instigator of kung fu at the original Shaolin temple.

Bok Hok Pai White crane style of kung fu.

Bokken Solid wooden sword used for training purposes.

Bok Mei Pai White eyebrow style of kung fu.

Buddhism Eastern religion which spread from India to China, then to many parts of Asia. Various branches or sects exist as offshoots.

Bushi Japanese term means 'warrior'.

Bushido or 'way of the warrior', a very strict samurai code of ethics based on honour, loyalty, duty, and obedience.

Butterfly Knives Also known as *bot jum do*. Short knives used in pairs in kung fu systems.

Centre Line Imaginary line running down the centre of the body, the location of many vital points.

Chan or Ch'an Chinese word for Zen the word means 'meditation'. In India it is known as *Dhyana*.

Chan San Feng Legendary founder of tai chi chuan, one of the internal schools of Chinese boxing.

Chi or Chi-Gung Internal energy; a special set of exercises to develop inner strength.

Chi Sao Exercise in wing chun kung fu for building co-ordination and sensitivity; also teaches correct elbow positioning.

Choy Li Fut Southern Chinese form of Shaolin kung fu.

Chuan Chinese term meaning 'fist'.

Chudan In Japanese martial arts, the middle area or chest.

Crane One of the five animal styles in Shaolin kung fu.

Dan Japanese term for anyone who has achieved the rank of black belt or higher.

Daruma Japanese name for the Indian monk Bodhidharma. Known as Ta-Mo in China.

Dim Mak The death touch. A delayed action strike that can kill a victim hours or days after the blow has been struck.

Do In Japanese means 'way' or 'path', identified with Chinese tao.

Dojo Training hall or place used for practising Japanese martial arts.

Dragon One of the five animal styles of Shaolin kung fu. The dragon symbolizes spirit.

Drunken Monkey System of kung fu in which a practitioner staggers to fool an opponent into thinking he is intoxicated.

Elbow Close quarter technique, used in martial arts. Also much favored by Thai boxers who know it as sok.

Empty Hand Literal meaning of karate in Japanese.

Escrima A Filipino martial art using sticks, swords, and daggers. The word is Spanish and means 'skirmish'. Also known as arnis de mano.

Five Ancestors The five survivors of the original Shaolin temple after it was sacked.

Form Series of choreographed movements incorporating many martial arts techniques. It is a set of patterns aimed at improving the practitioner's application of technique.

Free Fighting Exercise in all martial arts similar to sparring. A fighter uses his own interpretation of techniques to beat his opponent.

Full Contact A form of karate where full power kicks are delivered at an opponent. Contestants wear boxing gloves, and pads on their feet.

Gedan Lower area of the body, in Japanese martial arts.

Genin Lowest rank of the three classifications of the ninja. Genin were the ones who performed the assassinations.

Gi Training uniform used by practitioners of the Japanese martial arts. In karate it is known as a karate-gi, in judo a judo-gi.

Gichin Funakoshi founder of shotokan karate. He was instrumental in introducing karate into Japan from Okinawa.

Gojo-Ryu One of the major styles of karate developed from Okinawan naha-te. It is a hard and soft system.

Gung Fu common name for the Chinese martial arts, also pronounced kung fu.

Guru In pentjak-silat, the traditional teacher of the art. Of Muslim or Indian origin.

Hakama Long divided skirt covering the legs and feet. Used in aikido and many other Japanese martial arts.

Hapkido Korean martial art involving kicks and hand strikes, meaning 'the way of harmony'.

Hara-Kiri Japanese ritual suicide by disembowelment. Proper term is seppuku.

Honbu Headquarters of the different Japanese martial arts.

Hsing-I Chinese soft or internal kung fu art.

Hung Gar One of the five ancestor styles of kung fu.

Hwarang Do 'The way of the flowering manhood'. A code similar to bushido used in Korea by members of the Hwarang. Hwarang-do is not a much practised martial art.

Hyung One of the basics of taekwon-do training; the practice of forms or patterns.

Iai-Do Japanese martial art of drawing and re-sheathing the *katana* or sword. It is a noncombat art descended from iai-jutsu. It stresses intellectual and spiritual attainment.

I-Ching The Chinese *Book of Changes.* This ancient book is consulted even today for telling the future. The teachings of the I-Ching form the philosophical basis of tai chi chuan.

Iga An area in Japan known for its remoteness in medieval times. Home of one of the many school of ninja.

Iron Palm Lethal technique known in kung fu for its ability to kill with a single blow. Much conditioning is required over several years to made the adept's hand and arm like iron. Not to be confused with dim mak.

Jiu-Jitsu Ancient Japanese form of warrior training, including both armed and unarmed techniques. The term means 'soft' or 'flexible'.

Jodan In Japanese martial arts, the top area of the body, i.e. from the shoulders upwards.

Jonin Highest rank in the ninja echelon.

Judo Modern sport form of jiu-jitsu. Developed by Dr Jigoro Kano in 1882. The sport form uses the opponent's own strength to his disadvantage.

Judoka One who practises judo.

Jutsu Japanese word meaning 'skill' or 'art'.

Kalaripayit Indian method of combat. The term means 'battle place' or 'field'.

Kama The sickle, a weapon developed in Okinawa.

Karate Japanese martial art developed from Chinese systems. It is a means of self-defence for an unarmed person using strikes and kicks aimed at the body.

Karateka One who trains in karate.

Kata In karate, a pre-set series of movements in which the practitioner defends himself against imaginary opponents.

Kempo Japanese pronunciation of *chuan'fa,* which is Chinese for 'way of the fist'. Kempo is a type of Chinese and Korean karate based on high speed blocks and counterattacks.

Kendo Modern Japanese fencing based on the warrior skill of kenjutsu. In kendo practitioners fight with bamboo shinai.

Ki Japanese word for the internal intrinsic energy within the body. Ki is the Japanese translation of the Chinese chi. Ki is the inner power.

Krabi-Krabong Armed combat system of Thailand. Adepts fight with twin swords or sword and shield.

Kung Fu All the fighting arts of China. It is a slang generic term meaning 'a person of attainment', or 'one who works or exercises to the highest of his ability'. It was adopted erroneously by westerners then became accepted and used by the Chinese themselves.

Kup In taekwon-do, the eight grades of ranking before the black belt, comparable to the Japanese kyu. The lowest kup, that of a beginner, is eighth kup.

Kyudo 'Way of the bow'. Japanese martial art of archery with deep Zen concepts.

Lao Tzo or Tsu Legendary sage in Chinese history credited with founding Taoism. Author of the Chinese classic *The Tao Te Ching.*

Lo Han Name of any famous disciple of Buddha. A special series of exercises taught by Bodhidharma to the original monks at the Shaolin temple.

Marma-adi Secret teachings of striking the vital points in the Indian art of kalaripayit.

Martial art Pertaining to war arts, now means a fighting discipline to promote combat proficiency when unarmed or armed.

Mook Joong Wooden dummy, shaped like a man and used for conditioning and training purposes in many hard styles of kung fu.

Muay Thai Correct term for Thai boxing.

Naginata Japanese martial art, adopted mainly by women. Uses a spear with a curved blade about 3 feet long. In the modern combat sport form bamboo replaces the spear tip.

Naha Te One of the three original styles of Okinawan karate.

Ninja Secret society of mercenary assassins in Japan. It means 'stealers-in'. Trained from birth to become experts in death by assassination.

Ninjutsu Art or techniques of the ninja.

Nunchaku Two wooden batons linked by a short chain or cord to make an awesome weapon. Used originally as a rice flail in many parts of Southeast Asia.

Pa-Kua Internal style of kung fu, based on circular movements with open-palm hand strikes. It means 'eight trigrams' and the concept comes from the Chinese classic the *I Ching,* or book of changes.

Pentjak-Silat Indonesian martial art descended from Malaysian bersilat.

Praying Mantis Known in China as *tong long.* Named after Wong Long who invented the style after witnessing a fight between a grasshopper and a praying mantis.

Randori In judo, free practice or sparring where techniques are not prearranged.

Rokushakubo Okinawan 6 foot staff or pole made from oak or similar hardwood. *Roku* means 'six', *shaku* is about a foot length, *bo* means 'pole' or 'staff'.

Roundhouse Kick Kick used in virtually all martial arts. Its circular path gives it extra power from centrifugal force. It is probably one of the most powerful kicks in the martial artist's arsenal.

Ryu In Japanese martial arts, means 'school' or 'style'.

Sai Three-pronged forklike weapon once made of iron, now made of steel. Used mainly in karate for demonstration purposes. Resembles a very short blunt sword.

Samurai Japanese feudal warrior. The word means 'one who serves'. Likened to the medieval knights of Europe. A samurai served as a military retainer to the Daimyos and the Shogun. Samurai replaced the old word *bushi,* which means 'warrior'.

Savate Or *la savate,* French system of boxing and kicking related to Burmese bando and Thai boxing.

Sensei Japanese word for 'instructor' or 'teaching'.

Shaolin Temple in Honan in China where allegedly kung fu was born.

Shinai Bamboo sword made of four strips bound together. Used in Kendo.

Shinobi Old term from which the word ninja was derived.

Shorinji Kempo Japanese karate with very strong Chinese kung fu influences, founded by its now deceased headmaster Doshin So. The organization in Japan is now headed by his daughter.

Shotokan School of Japanese karate founded by Gichin Funakoshi in 1922. Probably the most widely practised style of karate in the world today.

Shuriken Throwing stars originally made of iron, sharply pointed and used by the ninja.

Sifu Instructor in kung fu; the word means 'father'.

Sil Lum Cantonese name for Shaolin.

Sport Karate Karate competition where contestants fight under combat rules in a ring or area. They wear protective gloves and foot pads. Techniques are scored and points are given. Actual contact is prohibited, although some leeway is allowed.

Sumo Ancient Japanese art of wrestling, steeped in quasi-religious aspects. Contestants build themselves up to great weights in order to gain an advantage.

Taekwon-do Or *taekwondo*, Korean style of empty hand combat very similar to Japanese karate. As in karate-do, great emphasis is place on strikes with hands and feet.

Tae Kyon Ancient Korean weaponless fighting art from which taekwon-do is said to be derived. Tae kyon officially became taekwon-do in 1945.

Tai Chi Chuan Or *tai chi* as it is more commonly known, one of the three major internal or soft arts of kung fu. Today more emphasis is placed on its therapeutic value to relieve stress and guide one into a state of tranquillity. The word means 'great or grand ultimate fist'.

Tamashiwara Japanese technique of using strikes with the body against materials such as wood, tiles, bricks, ice, etc, to test the power or force of a strike.

Tang Shou Do Korean term, an alternative name for Chinese boxing.

Tang Soo Do 'Way of the tang hand'. Korean martial

system similar to shotokan karate. Developed by Hwang Kee in 1949. Based on ancient Korean arts of t'ang su and subak.

Tao Chinese term mean 'path' or 'way'. Tao is an invisible force or energy present in all things in the universe.

Te Japanese term meaning 'hand'.

Thai Boxing *See* MUAY THAI.

Thaing General term for Burmese arts of self-defense.

Tobok Suit worn to practice taekwon-do, consisting of a loose shirt and pants tied with a sash or belt.

Tonfa Okinawan weapon, once the handle used to operate a manual millstone. Used in karate to improve technique. Also a similar device used in many US states as a police weapon to replace the now obsolete night stick or billy club.

White Belt In Japanese martial arts, colour of a beginner.

Wing Chun Kung fu system invented by a woman. System studied by the late Bruce Lee on which to base his own system of jeet kune-do. Based on the law of economy of movement.

Wu Shu Generic term for the martial arts of mainland China.

Yang In Chinese cosmology, the positive aspect of the universe. Yang relates to male and light, one half of the Taoist view of the universe; characterized by positive action.

Yari Japanese weapon, a straight spear about 8 ft long. It replaced the naginata as a battlefield weapon. So far as is known, the yari never evolved as a sporting 'do' form.

Yin In Chinese cosmology, the negative aspect of the universe. Relates to emptiness, softness, darkness, and female. Yin is the black fish with the white eye, in the famous Yin-Yang symbol.

Yudansha Kendoka who has achieve the rank of black belt or higher. Only those of yudansha rank are permitted to wear an outfit that is of uniform colour.

Zen Religious philosophy that claims that one can reach *satori,* or enlightenment, through meditation. Founded by the Indian monk Bodhidharma.
Zen makes use of illogical poems called *koans* to clear the mind of trivia and so reach the meditative state required. In China Zen is called *Ch'an.* Zen was much favoured by the Japanese Samurai.

Index

The author wishes to add his special thanks and appreciation to Mr Steve Hughes, Sales Manager, of Rockliff Computers Ltd, Manchester, England